14/12

Official Publisher Partnership

OCR PE for GCSE

John Honeybourne

HODDER
EDUCATION
AN HACHETTE UK COMPANY

Orders: please contact Bookpoint Ltd, 130 Milton Park, Abingdon, Oxon OX14 4SB. Telephone: (44) 01235 827720. Fax: (44) 01235 400454. Lines are open from 9.00–5.00, Monday to Saturday, with a 24-hour message answering service. You can also order through our website www.hoddereducation.co.uk.

British Library Cataloguing in Publication Data
A catalogue record for this title is available from the British Library

ISBN: 978 0 340 98330 0

First Published 2009
Impression number   10 9 8 7 6
Year   2014 2013 2012 2011

Hachette UK's policy is to use papers that are natural, renewable and recyclable products and made from wood grown in sustainable forests. The logging and manufacturing processes are expected to conform to the environmental regulations of the country of origin.

Cover photo Anne-Marie Weber © Corbis
Illustrations by Simon Tegg
Typeset by Pantek Arts Ltd, Maidstone, Kent
Printed in Dubai for Hodder Education, an Hachette UK Company, 338 Euston Road, London NW1 3BH

CONTENTS

ACKNOWLEDGEMENTS

The author and publishers wish to thank the following for permission to reproduce their images:

1.1	© Matthew Clarke/Action Plus
1.2	© Leo Mason/Action Plus
1.3	© Chris Barry/Action Plus
1.4	© Lutz Bongarts/Bongarts/Getty Images
1.5	© Chris Cole/Action Plus
1.6	© Christopher Bissell/Stone/Getty Images
2.1	© FABRICE COFFRINI/AFP/Getty Images
2.2	© Neil Tingle/Action Plus
2.3	© Glyn Kirk/Action Plus
2.4	© JEWEL SAMAD/AFP/Getty Images
2.5	© 2009 Robert Llewellyn/photolibrary.com
2.6	© 2009 Banana Stock / photolibrary.com
2.7	© Glyn Kirk/Action Plus
2.8	© Action Plus
2.9	© Radius Images/Alamy
2.10	© Clive Brunskill/Getty Images
2.11 (left)	© Michael Steele/Getty Images
2.11 (right)	© JUPITERIMAGES/ Polka Dot/Alamy
2.12	© Michael Krasowitz/Photographer's Choice/Getty Images
2.13 (left)	© Mike Powell/Allsport /Getty Images
2.13 (right)	© Johner/Getty Images
3.1	© JUPITERIMAGES/BananaStock/Alamy
3.2	© Doug Benc/Getty Images
3.3	© Julian Finney/Getty Images
3.4	© HOW HWEE YOUNG/epa/Corbis
3.5	© GLYN KIRK/AFP/Getty Images
4.1.1	© Glyn Kirk/Action Plus
4.1.2	© Steve Bardens/Action Plus
4.1.3	© JUPITERIMAGES/BananaStock/Alamy
4.1.4 (left)	© imagebroker/Alamy
4.1.4 (right)	© Henry Westheim Photography/Alamy
4.1.5	© Peter Cade Iconica /Getty Images
4.1.6	© Peter Cade/Iconica/Getty Images
4.1.7	© Action Plus
4.2.7 (right)	© ADRIAN DENNIS/AFP/Getty Images
4.2.8	© Neil Tingle/Action Plus
4.2.9	© Neil Tingle/Action Plus
4.2.10	© Neal and Molly Jansen/Alamy
4.2.11	© Wally McNamee/CORBIS
4.2.14	© AGStockUSA, Inc./Alamy
4.3.2	© Steve Bardens/Action Plus
4.3.4	© Custom Medical Stock Photo/Alamy

Introduction

GCSE Physical Education for the OCR examination board is a subject that encourages you to understand the importance of following an active and healthy lifestyle. *OCR PE for GCSE* is a comprehensive textbook that will help you in your studies for GCSE Physical Education. Split into two sections, the book closely follows the format of the OCR exam specification and also the likely course route taken by your teachers in their schemes of work.

If you are studying the long course for GCSE Physical Education, you will find all the content of *OCR PE for GCSE* is suitable for you. If you are following the short course option, the short course content is well signposted within *OCR PE for GCSE* by the use of the short course icon. Simply follow this icon (SC) throughout the text.

Section 1 covers the key concepts and key processes of Physical Education, and includes chapters on developing skills and techniques, decision-making in the different roles as participant, official and leader, physical and mental capacity to fulfil the requirements of these roles, evaluating and improving and, finally, healthy, active lifestyles.

Section 2 covers the opportunities and pathways for involvement in physical activity, and includes chapters on the levels of participation, reasons for participation and non-participation, specific social, cultural and locational factors affecting participation, school influences on participation, and the identification and description of pathways for involvement in physical activity.

Success in examinations is a combination of your teacher's expertise, your own motivation and ability as a student, and accessibility to the appropriate resources — including a relevant textbook! Written by an expert examiner, *OCR PE for GCSE* is highly relevant and contains resources that will not only support and help you to prepare thoroughly for your exams, but also stretch and challenge you at whatever level of ability you are now. Examination questions for this specification often ask for theoretical knowledge and understanding to be put into a practical context. *OCR PE for GCSE* relates theory well with practice, and provides you with a wealth of practical examples that increase your understanding of the theoretical principles underlying physical activity.

Within *OCR PE for GCSE* you will find that every chapter offers a wide range of learning resources, with each resource signposted throughout by a distinctive icon in the text. These are:

 Learning goals to keep you on track with the requirements of the OCR exam specification

 Examiner's tips to provide you with good examples of all-important exam techniques

 Activities, including *Tasks* for you to complete whatever your level of ability and *Challenges* to stretch you and encourage you to be more analytical in your approach — thus helping you to aim for the top marks necessary to gain the top grades

Key words that provide you with clear definitions of complex physiological and technical phrases

 Exam-style questions, such as *multi-choice* and *short answer questions*, to prepare you for the types of questions you can expect in the GCSE exam

 Review questions to check your understanding of the topics already covered in the chapter you have just read

 'What you need to know' sections to help you during revision to check that you have the necessary information under your belt

 Practical applications that give you lots of practical examples of theory being demonstrated in physical activities

 Useful websites to top up your knowledge in important areas of the OCR specification

OCR PE for GCSE is written in a clear, highly readable way that will help you to understand and learn about Physical Education. By using the materials within *OCR PE for GCSE* you will be well on your way to preparing not just for your OCR exam, but also for a healthy, active life.

John Honeybourne

2009

Teaching the long or short course

To ensure that you and your students are following the correct pathway for the Short Course for the OCR GCSE specification, please see the table below.

CHAPTER	SUITABLE FOR LONG COURSE	SUITABLE FOR SHORT COURSE
1 An introduction to the concepts and processes in physical education	✓	✓
2 Developing skills and techniques	✓	✓ However, students do not need to study: • methods of learning skills • different types of feedback in learning skills • how feedback helps to motivate participants in physical activities
3 Decision making in different roles	✓	✓
4.1 Components of fitness	✓	✓
4.2 How physical activity impacts on the development of the skeletal system	✓	
4.3 The ways in which an active, healthy lifestyle can affect muscles	✓	
5 Evaluating and improving	✓	✓
6.1 Healthy, active lifestyles	✓	✓
6.2 Healthy, active lifestyles in practice	✓	
7 Levels of participation in sport and physical activity	✓	✓ However, students need only know about: • the levels of participation in physical activities for different age groups • the number of people who regularly participate in physical activity
8 Reasons for participation and non-participation in physical activities	✓	✓ However, students need only be able to identify and explain: • the reasons for participation in physical activity • the reasons for non-participation in physical activity
9 Specific social, cultural and locational factors affecting participation	✓	✓ However, students do not need to be able to describe a range of government initiatives that promote a healthy, active lifestyle

CHAPTER	SUITABLE FOR LONG COURSE	SUITABLE FOR SHORT COURSE
10 School influences on participation	✓	✓ *However, students need only be able to describe:* • *The role of the school curriculum in promoting a healthy, active lifestyle* • *The processes of Key Stages 3 & 4 with examples for physical education in schools*
11 Identification and description of pathways for involvement in physical activity	✓	✓

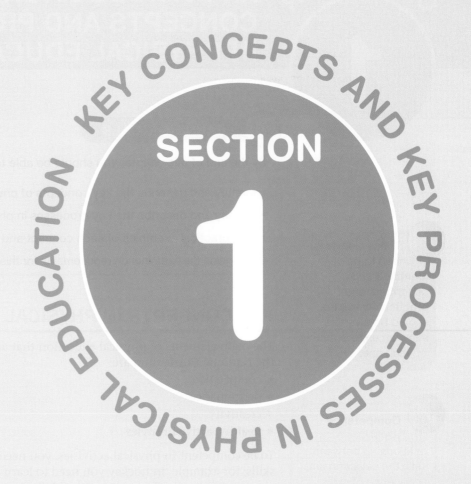

SECTION 1

KEY CONCEPTS AND KEY PROCESSES IN PHYSICAL EDUCATION

1

AN INTRODUCTION TO THE CONCEPTS AND PROCESSES IN PHYSICAL EDUCATION

LEARNING GOALS

By the end of this chapter you should be able to:

- identify and describe the key concepts of physical education (SC)
- identify and describe the key processes in physical education (SC)
- give practical examples of each concept and process (SC)
- recognise the examination requirements for this section of the specification (SC)

 These elements need to be **identified** and **described**, and **practical examples** should be given to show an understanding of each one.

✓ **Competence**
This is the relationship between skill, the selection and application of skills, tactics and compositional ideas and the readiness of body and mind to cope with physical activity.

Fig 1.1 To be competent in hockey you need to have learned the appropriate skills (for example, how to stop and hit the ball)

KEY CONCEPTS IN PHYSICAL EDUCATION

The main elements of physical education that are required to be studied as part of the National Curriculum are:

- competence
- performance
- creativity
- healthy, active lifestyles

To be competent in physical activities, you need to have learned the appropriate skills; for example, in hockey you need to learn how to stop and hit a ball. You also need to know when to use these skills; for example, in basketball to know when to shoot. Another element of competence is to use appropriate tactics in the activity; for example, in football to know when to concentrate on attacking and when to put your efforts into defending. In some activities you also need to use ideas to link movements together; for example, in a gymnastics routine. You also need to be fit enough to do the activity effectively; for example, you should not get out of breath too easily when playing a team game. Finally, to be competent you need to have the right mental approach; for example, in an exercise class you need to show determination to finish the class.

The concept of performance in physical education is about how well a task related to physical activities is completed. Your performance can be good, average or poor depending on many different factors. To perform well you need to be physically able and have good skills; for example, if you are in the school netball team you can probably run fast over a short distance and change direction well. You also need to know what is required to perform your skills well; for example, if you are in the school football team you can probably read the game well and make appropriate runs at the right time. If your physical skills and your knowledge and understanding of the game are all good then you are likely to perform well and achieve success; for example, if you are a good rugby player you are likely to tackle well and pass the ball effectively to other team mates to win games.

The concept of creativity in physical education is concerned with using your imagination and trying things out before deciding the best course of action. You might try different techniques in the long jump; for example, and when you find the technique to suit your own abilities you will practise that technique in order

Performance
Using physical competence and knowledge and understanding of physical activity to produce effective outcomes when participating in physical activity.

Fig 1.2 Performance is a concept that involves your physical and mental abilities

Creativity
Exploring and experimenting with techniques, tactics and compositional ideas to produce efficient and effective outcomes.

Healthy, active lifestyles
Understanding the positive contribution that regular, fit for purpose physical activity makes to the physical and mental health of the individual.

to be successful. You might try different tactics in badminton to see which one is the most effective and scores the most points; for example, by playing close to the net or at the back of the court. In more creative activities such as dance you might use your imagination to create a dance that represents an object, experience or emotional feeling; for example, a dance to show the effects of drugs or a dance to show anger or joy.

The concept of a healthy, active lifestyle is very important in physical education. In many classroom activities and sports you may recognise the link between physical activity and health. You need to understand that if you exercise regularly this may help you to become not only fitter in your body but also happier in yourself. It is well known that physical activity can cause chemicals to be released that make us feel happier and less anxious. It is also important for the activities you participate in to be the right type for you; for example, if you enjoy being with others and are competitive then a team game could well be an appropriate activity for you. Regular exercise is well known for keeping the body fit and less prone to illness.

ACTIVITY 1

TASK
Identify all the key concepts for physical education. Give a practical example for each.

CHALLENGE
Take one activity and show that you understand the key concepts by giving an example from your activity for each concept; for example, if you are a keen volleyball player you may show creativity (one of the concepts above) in developing a fake smash (or spike) to outwit your opponent.

Fig 1.3 A volleyball player may show creativity in developing a fake smash to outwit his/her opponent

*You should be able to **identify** (name each process), **describe** (give the main characteristics) and give **practical examples** of each process.*

KEY PROCESSES IN PHYSICAL EDUCATION

The key processes in PE are the essential physical and mental skills that pupils need to learn in order to make progress. The key processes are:

- developing skills and techniques
- decision making
- physical and mental capacity
- evaluating and improving
- making informed choices about active, healthy lifestyles.

Developing skills in physical activity

You should be able to refine and adapt skills into techniques; for example, to develop the technique of serving in tennis you need to co-ordinate the throw up of the ball, and your body and arm movements to strike the ball. This process also involves developing the range of skills you use; for example, if you are involved in circuit training you may need to learn different skills for each activity in the circuit. Development of precision, control and fluency in skills is also an aspect of this process; for example, in basketball your shooting will be more accurate and your arm action in the shot more fluid if you practise hard each day.

Making and applying decisions

You should be able to select and use tactics, strategies and compositional ideas effectively in different creative, competitive and challenge-type contexts; for example, choosing the right skills to show the judges in a trampolining competition.

Fig 1.4 Choosing the right skills to show the judges in a trampolining competition is an example of effective decision making.

www.qca.org.uk
The website of the Qualifications and Curriculum Authority (QCA), which oversees the PE curriculum in schools, provides more details of the PE curriculum.

www.youthsportstrust.org
Gives more information on the Key Stage 3 curriculum and how it promotes participation.

In this process you should be able to refine and adapt ideas and plans in response to changing circumstances; for example, if you are losing in a game of squash you might try more defensive strategies. This process also requires you to plan and implement what needs practising so as to be more effective in performance; for example, to choose a particular skill such as tackling to practise in rugby training. Recognising hazards and making decisions about how to control any risks to yourself and others is another important aspect of this process; for example, if you were to find broken glass on a football pitch you would need to postpone the start of the game until the hazard had been removed.

Developing physical and mental capacity

This process means developing the physical strength, stamina, speed and flexibility to cope with the demands of different activities; for example, following a fitness programme that gives good all-round fitness benefits. It also involves the mental determination to succeed; for example, having enough motivation to attend a challenging exercise class.

Fig 1.5 The process of developing physical and mental capacity is being able to develop the physical strength, stamina, speed and flexibility to cope with the demands of the activity

Evaluating and improving

This process involves being able to analyse performance in physical activities and identify strengths and weaknesses; for example, watching a tennis player and identifying a fault in the performer's forehand but also recognising that they have a good serve. It also involves making decisions about how to improve your own and others' performance and acting on these decisions; for example, recognising that you are weak in shooting in football and planning to improve your shooting technique in training. For the purposes of evaluation and improvement it is important to be clear about what the performer wants to achieve in their own work and what they have actually achieved.

Fig 1.6 The process of evaluating and improving involves being able to analyse performance in physical activities and identify strengths and weaknesses

Making informed choices about healthy, active lifestyles

This process is about being able to identify the types of physical activity that are best suited to you and the types of role you might like to take on; for example, as a player or a coach or a referee. It also involves making choices about involvement in healthy physical activity; for example, choosing an activity that may help with strengthening your heart, such as long-distance running.

PRACTICAL APPLICATIONS

These key processes are identified and developed by schools in their curriculum for all pupils in years 10 and 11 (called Key Stage 4)

DEVELOPING SKILLS IN PHYSICAL ACTIVITY
Students should be able to:
- improve the range, difficulty and quality of their skills and techniques
- develop the consistency with which they use and perform skills with precision, control and fluency.

MAKING AND APPLYING DECISIONS
Students should be able to:
- select and use tactics, strategies and compositional ideas imaginatively in complex and demanding creative, competitive and challenge-type contexts
- design original and effective plans that improve their own and others' performance
- respond effectively and imaginatively to changing circumstances as they arise during a performance.
- organise and manage the environment they are working in to ensure the health, safety and well-being of themselves and others.

DEVELOPING PHYSICAL AND MENTAL CAPACITY
Students should be able to:
- analyse how mental and physical capacity affects performance
- maintain and develop their physical strength, stamina, speed and flexibility

to cope with the demands of different activities and active lifestyles
- prepare mentally for successful involvement in physical activity, performance and engagement in healthy, active lifestyles.

EVALUATING AND IMPROVING
Students should be able to:
- critically evaluate, analyse and judge the quality and effectiveness of performances
- make informed decisions about how to improve the quality and effectiveness of their own and others' performances
- develop and implement imaginative action plans to improve the quality and effectiveness of performances
- design original and effective plans that improve the quality of their own and others' involvement in healthy, active lifestyles.

MAKING INFORMED CHOICES ABOUT HEALTHY, ACTIVE LIFESTYLES
Students should be able to:
- identify the types of physical activity available to them and the roles they would like to take on
- link physical activity with diet, work and rest for personal health and well-being
- make informed decisions about getting involved in a lifetime of healthy physical activities that suit their needs.

ACTIVITY 2

ACTIVITY 2

TASK

For each of the following 'processes' give a practical example of this taking place in your school:
- developing skills (e.g. teaching hockey skills)
- making and applying decisions (a pupil umpiring a netball match in a PE lesson)
- developing physical and mental capacity (pupil as leader running a year 8 football session)

- evaluating and improving (a fellow pupil assessing your performance in gymnastics)
- making informed decisions about lifestyle (in a GCSE theory session, being taught about healthy eating).

CHALLENGE
- Write a short essay for the Head of PE outlining an idea to develop each of the above processes.

 REVIEW QUESTIONS

1 What are the key concepts for physical education?
2 What examples of each concept can you give?
3 What are the key processes?
4 What examples of each process can you give?

 EXAM-STYLE QUESTIONS

Multiple choice questions
1 Which of the following is a physical education concept?
   a frequency of training
   b warm-up
   c creativity
   d decision making.

2 Which of the following is the best example of evaluating and improving as a process in physical education?
   a watching a tennis player and identifying a fault in the performer's forehand and then showing them a better technique
   b watching a hockey player and cheering them on, urging them to improve
   c watching a gymnastics sequence and telling them the judges' score at the end
   d watching an exercise class and telling them they have to try harder next time.

Short answer questions
1 Describe the concept of performance in physical education, giving practical examples throughout your answer. **(4 marks)**
2 What is meant by the decision-making process in physical education? **(3 marks)**
3 Identify and explain three processes in physical education and describe an activity where all three may be shown. **(6 marks)**

 WHAT YOU NEED TO KNOW

- how to identify and describe the key concepts of physical education
- how to identify and describe the key processes in physical education
- how to give practical examples of each concept and each process.

CHAPTER 2

DEVELOPING SKILLS AND TECHNIQUES

 LEARNING GOALS

By the end of this chapter you should be able to:

- explain what is meant by 'fundamental motor skills' and give practical examples
- describe and explain methods in which skills are learned
- explain the importance of different types of feedback in learning skills
- explain how feedback helps to motivate participants in physical activities
- describe and explain 'intrinsic' and 'extrinsic motivation' with examples
- relate motivation to the different roles of participant, leader and official
- explain the importance of goal setting in performance, participation and to control anxiety
- describe the SMART principle of goal setting.

The specification demands that you are able to describe these skills and also to show how each can be measured and analysed. Use your experience in practical lessons to help you with these descriptions.

✓ **Fundamental motor skills**

These are skills such as throwing or kicking a ball or jumping. We learn these skills at a young age, usually through play and, if they are learned thoroughly, we can move on to the more sophisticated actions that are required in sport.

FUNDAMENTAL MOTOR SKILLS

When a good football player, for instance, performs a skilful pass, he or she shows a technically good movement. This movement is called a *motor skill*.

Fundamental motor skills are skills such as throwing, catching and running. These skills are important because they provide the basis for other skills. Without acquiring the fundamental motor skills, it is unlikely that a person would be able to excel in a sports activity. These skills provide the platform on which we can build the more advanced skills demanded in our sports. Acquisition of these essential skills also helps us to follow a lifestyle that is healthy. As we get older, we may draw on many fundamental motor skills to follow lifetime sports, such as golf. Acquiring fundamental motor skills can help children build their self-esteem and make them more accepted in group 'play' situations.

Running

Running is often developed during the 'toddler years' and is the basis of many types of physical activities. Running can be analysed through technique or the style of the movements the participant uses to run. This technique is often dependent upon whether fast short-distance running is required or longer running.

Poor running technique can lead to unnecessary injury risks if it is not picked up early. Many recreational runners and those even just running for a bus are placing undue strain on their bodies, as well as reducing their speed, by using the wrong technique. Whether you run to keep fit, compete at the Olympics or participate at any level in a multidirectional ball sport you can always improve your running and sprinting technique.

Fig 2.1 Running well and running fast is a skill, not something you were born with. And, just like any other skill, it can be taught

Running well and running fast is a skill, not something you were born with. And just like any other skill it can be taught. Some weaknesses in runners and joggers are:

- bouncing up and down too much
- over striding
- not using their hamstrings enough
- landing on feet too heavily
- breaking action on landing
- not using arms
- twisting midriff side to side while running
- the head and upper body are bent forward
- jogging too slowly.

All accomplished and elite runners run on the balls of their feet. The foot should strike the surface with the ball of the foot, in a dorsiflexed position (with toes pointing forward not downwards). The heel doesn't touch the ground.

Assessment of running is often through timing. In sport it may be over a specific distance, e.g. 100 metres or a marathon of over 26 miles.

The following are examples of world records for different distances (September 2008)

- 100 metres sprint (male) – 9.69 seconds: U. Bolt (Jamaica)
- 100 metres sprint (female) – 10.49 seconds: F.G. Joyner (USA)
- marathon (male) – 2hours 4 minutes and 26 seconds: H. Gebrselassie (Ethiopia)
- marathon (female) – 2 hours 15 minutes and 25 seconds: P. Radcliffe (GB)

Throwing

This fundamental movement skill is essential for many physical activities, especially those involving a ball. The throwing action does not just apply to throwing a ball from one person to another but can be transferred to a variety of activities; for example, in tennis the serve involves a throwing action.

Throwing competitions and other track and field events, including shot put and discus, originated in Greece over 2,000 years ago. As track and field events evolved, the hammer and javelin have been added to the list of throwing sports.

Throwing athletes may not look like they have a lot of strength, especially shot putters, who are generally tall but heavy, while javelin throwers tend to be very thin, like runners. Success is not so much a matter of sheer brute force as of effective technique.

Throwing can cause damage unless the correct technique is used. Many who throw as part of a physical activity are at risk from over-use injury to muscle tissues, especially around the upper limb joints, with the lower back and knees also being areas of concern.

The best way to avoid throwing-sport injuries is to limit or restrict the number of throws you make during each exercise or training session.

Shot put is one of the original throwing events and the sport has moved from a very basic action to one that is now specific to each particular athlete. There are many different styles of throwing used in shot put, with the 180-degree shot, developed by Perry O'Brien, being more effective than the originally used 90-degree action. O'Brien discovered the longer he pushed, the faster the shot would travel.

In an effort to avoid injury, shot putters must not only use the proper technique, but also do a lot of arm, waist, hamstring, hip and quadriceps stretching, as those are the areas used most by these athletes.

The shot should also not be too heavy for the thrower. Always throw on a flat, dry surface – this will help avoid ankle injuries.

The javelin, which has its roots in hunting and warfare, is a spear-like object made of metal, fibreglass or carbon fibre.

Although the sport has only been a part of the Summer Olympics since 1908, the javelin was a part of the ancient Olympics. The original objective was to throw the javelin at a target, whereas nowadays it is to throw the longest possible distance.

Learning the proper throwing technique will go a long way towards increasing the distance thrown and avoiding injury. The thrower must throw over the shoulder or upper part of the throwing arm, while leading and throwing with the elbows in order to avoid injury. A javelin must never be slung or hurled. As with shot put, it is important for a correctly weighted javelin to be used.

Assessment of throwing is often through measuring the distance of the object thrown.

World records for shot put:

- R Barnes (male): 23.12 metres (USA) 1990
- N Lisovskaya (female): 22.63 metres (USSR) 1987.

Fig 2.2 In an effort to avoid injury, shot putters must use proper technique

Kicking

This fundamental motor skill is used in a variety of physical activities, the most common of which is football. Again, the correct technique and accuracy are the most important elements of this action.

Football kicking techniques include basic shooting and passing skills up to advanced techniques such as bending the ball around a wall and overhead kicks. The basic kicking skill uses the instep for kicking at goal and passing the football. The instep, the part of the foot where the laces are, provides both power and control. The most common mistake made by beginners is to use the toe. Not only is this painful if somebody tackles hard when you are trying to kick, but it is also inaccurate. The advantage of the instep is that it presents a flat surface to the ball, and can also be used to make the ball swerve and dip.

The 'non-kicking' leg provides support, and should be slightly bent as you kick. When we want to keep the ball on the ground, the head is down, over the ball. The follow-through should be long and smooth.

Fig 2.3 The correct kicking technique is important for control and accuracy

Fig 2.3 The correct kicking technique is important for control and accuracy

Jumping

This fundamental motor skill is an event in its own right (for example, long jump or high jump) but it is also a basic requirement for many physical activities and sports. Young children start to jump up and down as soon as they are standing.

Basic long-jump technique

High speed, an accurate take-off and an explosive springy jump are the important elements of a successful long jump. The first half of the run-up should be rhythmic and relaxed. About halfway down, the arms and legs are pumped like a sprinter to get maximum speed as you hit the board. Your speed will give you the momentum needed to achieve a good 'flight' and a long jump. On take-off, drive your leading leg upward.

It is important to help force your body through the air by circling your arms. This action will also combat the forward rotation that naturally occurs after take-off. To delay landing, thrust both legs outward in their extended position and drive your hands down. This will thrust your shoulders and head forward.

Fig 2.4 High speed, an accurate take-off and an explosive springy jump are the important elements of a successful long jump

On landing, bend your knees and move your upper body forward as you hit the sand. To get a longer jump and prevent yourself from falling backwards, lean to one side as you land, using one elbow for balance. After landing, remember that walking back through the sand pit will get you disqualified in a competition.

The fundamental motorskill of jumping is assessed by measuring the height or the distance of the jump. The World record for long jump:

● M. Powell (male): 8.95 metres (USA) 1991
● G. Chistyakova: 7.52 metres (USSR) 1988.

Hitting

This is a very general fundamental motor skill that can be used in a wide range of physical activities and sports. Examples include cricket, rounders, tennis, etc.

Hitting involves the use of a hitting implement – usually some sort of bat or racket. Therefore this action often requires good co-ordination. Hitting another person is the main element of boxing and this involves a great deal of technique over and beyond the basic hitting action.

Hitting a tennis ball – basic technique

The forehand stroke in tennis is an example of a fundamental motor skill being developed into a technique for a sport. It is easy to get it wrong – with some players hitting their forehand with the racquet head low, almost perpendicular to the ground, and swinging low to high with a big swing to try and get the topspin. A more effective technique keeps the racquet head above your wrist when hitting forehand and keeping the wrist firm. This gives you more control of your shot and you should also follow through with your racket.

Fig 2.5 The fundamental motor skill of hitting can be developed into a highly technical movement such as a tennis stroke

LEARNING MOVEMENT SKILLS

There are various definitions of learning but the predominant view is that experience gives us knowledge, which in turn influences the way we behave. Motor skills that are used in sports and physical activities as part of a healthy, active lifestyle are learned in a variety of different ways. Three of the main ways are:

● by making associations or links between what we see and hear (stimuli) and what we can do (response) by practising or rehearsing actions
● by using processes of trial and error
● by observing others and then copying them.

Practice and rehearsal

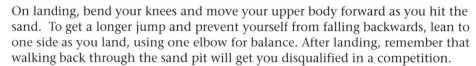

PRACTICAL APPLICATIONS

A child is learning to swim but shows fear of the water. The child has already learned the response of fear to the stimulus of the water. If the teacher ensures that the child experiences fun and enjoyment during the trip to the swimming pool, then the child may well develop a much more positive response to water. The association of fear with water will be replaced with a response showing enjoyment if the stimulus of water is associated with having fun.

Fig 2.6 Swimming can be fun!

When learning motor skills for physical activities we often **practise** repetitive drills that encourage movements to become almost automatic. The responses of the learner become **conditioned** when associated with a particular stimulus. A possible problem with the 'drill' style of teaching motor skills is that the participant does not gain an understanding of why he or she is doing something. This lack of understanding can limit the learning and development of further more complex skills.

This 'conditioning' by rehearsing and practising is more likely to succeed if there is a reward. This is often called **positive reinforcement**.

PRACTICAL APPLICATIONS

A hockey player dribbling the ball recognises a route opening to the goal and runs into that opening to take a shot at the goal in an almost automatic response.

This response has been practised many times in training when the stimulus of the opening becomes apparent.

Fig 2.7 Having practised shooting for goal in training, a hockey player can improve her performance under pressure

Trial and error learning of motor skills

Trial and error learning, sometimes called operant conditioning, involves the shaping of behaviour through the use of reinforcement.

If a reward is given when a certain behaviour takes place then learning is much faster; this is called complete reinforcement. Research shows that if a reward is given after a number of correct responses then learning takes longer but lasts longer; this is known as partial reinforcement. Trial and error learning is widely used in the teaching of motor skills and is extremely effective. Rewards are used extensively in skills teaching because they reinforce the type of behaviour required.

PRACTICAL APPLICATIONS

If you wished to teach a deep serve in tennis, you might draw a large chalk circle at the back of the opposing service box and ask the learner to try to serve into the chalk circle. After numerous practice sessions, which would be increasingly successful, you would draw a smaller circle and encourage the learner to serve into the smaller target. When success has been experienced at this new task, the circle could be removed altogether. The

learner is now 'conditioned' to serve a deep serve. This is an example of the operant method of conditioning. The target became progressively more demanding and realistic to the 'real' game situation. The correct responses of the learner may have been reinforced by the reward of praise that shaped the learner's behaviour. The actions were also reinforced through the learner's success at hitting the target.

Fig 2.8 A tennis serve can be improved through practice

Positive reinforcement

This is the name given to the use of reward to encourage behaviour to be repeated and to make learning more likely. The desire to receive more reward causes the behaviour to be repeated. Positive reinforcement in the teaching and learning of motor skills can be in a number of forms such as praise from the teacher when the learner makes a required response. There is wide use of merit badges when certain skills or levels of performance are attained.

PRACTICAL APPLICATIONS

Badges are given when specific distances are achieved in swimming. Swimming a length of the pool would result in a badge being given to the learner. The learner would experience pride and a sense of success through achieving the distance and might be motivated to swim it again and strive for more rewards for longer distances.

Fig 2.9 With positive reinforcement a swimmer's enjoyment and motivation can be increased

Others have argued that punishment is very effective in modifying behaviour but this can have detrimental side effects such as anxiety, lack of motivation and depression. Some argue that punishment merely suppresses a response rather than a response being unlearned and as soon as the punishment ceases the undesired response recurs. It is likely that a combination of reinforcement and punishment is effective with human behaviour.

Copying others – observational learning

Many believe that behaviour is learned in social situations and that responses are not just linked to association but are also influenced by other people. Learning takes place through the observation and copying or imitation of others. The person whose behaviour is being observed is called the **role model** and observational learning is often referred to as **modelling.** With observational learning, responses are spontaneous and often there is no intention on the model's part to be teaching any type of behaviour. Behaviour is more likely to be copied if the consequences of the behaviour both by the model and the observer are desirable. Therefore reinforcement is present but it is not as mechanical and thoughtless as conditioning theories propose.

Observational learning is not just about imitation; it also involves learning about morals, values and patterns of social behaviour.

A number of conclusions have been reached in studies about copying behaviour to learn motor skills:

- If the model shows behaviour that is more appropriate according to accepted behaviour, it is more likely to be copied; for example, aggressive male models are more likely to be copied than aggressive female models.
- The relevance of the model's behaviour is important. Boys are more likely to imitate the aggressive model than girls, because boys through influences around them such as the media or their friends often see aggressive behaviour as appropriate for them.
- Role models whose behaviour is reinforced in some way by significant others are likely to be copied.
- More powerful role models (or those who are perceived to be more powerful) are more likely to be imitated.
- If a role model's behaviour is consistent, it is more likely to be copied.

Social learning through observation and imitation is very relevant to learning motor skills in physical activities. Many of us find ourselves in situations where we can influence the views and behaviour of others, especially children; this may be because we are in a position of authority or because we are good at a particular sport. Top sports people sometimes forget that they are enthusiastically watched by many young viewers who will try to copy their every move – they are role models, whose behaviour is seen as acceptable and preferable to others.

When teaching skills, it is the demonstration process that is particularly important.

Demonstrations are very important in the acquisition of new skills. Imitation of the demonstration depends on the observer's attention, visualisation, retention, motor reproduction and motivation.

Retention

For a visual image to be stored permanently, there must be rehearsal and good memory organisation. Storing is known as 'retention'.

Paying attention

To be able to imitate or copy a demonstration, the performer must pay attention to the demonstration and focus on important movements or cues. The attractiveness, competence and status of the role model will influence the amount of attention they are paid. The personal characteristics of the observer and the incentives that are present are also important influences. If there are problems in copying the learned behaviour, it is often because attention had been distracted or interfered with at the time of watching the role model.

Recording a visual image

The observer must be able to remember the model that is presented. Therefore he or she needs to create a mental picture of the process. This is often referred to as a **visual image.** Mental rehearsal can improve retention of this mental image.

Fig 2.10 A gymnast demonstrating the correct way to do a handstand

Motor reproduction

The observer must be physically able to imitate the skill being observed. There must be a number of trials to get the feel of the skill via intrinsic feedback (there's more about feedback below). In older children, for example, there is more muscular development so it is more likely for the model's behaviour to be copied in more complex actions.

Motivation

The level of motivation of the observer is very important if behaviour is to be observed and copied. External reinforcement of the model will increase the motivation to imitate it, because the perceived consequences will be desirable.

We copy the skills performed by others because we are motivated to achieve success and because of our drive to be accepted by others. The coach or teacher could be viewed as a 'significant other', and as a role model worthy of being copied.

> The specification links feedback to the motivation of participants in physical activities. You should be able to show how feedback can encourage participants to follow an active, healthy lifestyle.

PRACTICAL APPLICATIONS

If a coach or teacher of gymnastics wants to demonstrate the handstand, or use another performer to demonstrate, it is best if:

- the demonstrator/model is successful/ significant in status
- aspects of the demonstration are highlighted, such as the position of the arms (attention)
- the demonstration is repeated and the observer's mental picture (visualisation) is stored permanently (retention)
- the activity is then practised and rehearsed, with support at first (motor reproduction)
- there are rewards available such as praise to encourage replication of the model or a badge to show that the skill has been learned (motivation).

THE USE OF FEEDBACK IN LEARNING MOTOR SKILLS

Feedback can be given during the performance of a motor skill or after its completion. Feedback is most effective if it is given close to the performance so the performance is fresh in the participant's mind. Feedback motivates, changes performance or actually reinforces learning. The more precise the feedback, then the more beneficial it is.

There are several forms of feedback:

- continuous feedback – feedback during the performance, either from the coach, instructor or teacher or from the continuous feel of the skill
- terminal feedback – feedback after the response has been completed
- knowledge of results – terminal feedback that gives the performer information about the end result of the response
- knowledge of performance – information about how well the movement is being executed, rather than the end result
- internal/intrinsic feedback – continuous feedback that comes from the **proprioceptors**
- external/extrinsic/augmented feedback – feedback that comes from external sources; for example, from sound or vision
- positive feedback – reinforces skill learning and gives information about a successful outcome
- negative feedback – information about an unsuccessful outcome, which can be used to build more successful strategies
- Two of these types of feedback are more important than the others in sports performance: **knowledge of results** and **knowledge of performance.**

Knowledge of results

This feedback is external, and can come from the performer seeing the result of their response, or from another person – usually a coach or teacher. It is extremely important for the performer to know what the result of their action has been. There can be very little learning without this type of feedback, especially in the early stages of skill acquisition.

Knowledge of performance

This is feedback about the pattern of movement that has taken, or is taking, place. It is normally associated with external feedback but can be gained through **kinaesthetic awareness**, especially if the performer is highly skilled and knows what a good performance feels like.

 PRACTICAL APPLICATIONS

Both knowledge of results and knowledge of performance can help with the motivation of a performer, but if used incorrectly they can also demotivate. If, for example, negative feedback were given to a beginner at tennis, such as 'You were no good and your technique was all wrong', this would probably lead them to give up.

Reinforcement is essential for effective skill learning, and feedback serves as a good reinforcer. If the movement and/or the result is good then the performer will feel satisfaction. Knowing that the movement and results are good will help the performer to form a picture of what is correct and to associate future performance with that picture, image or model.

External feedback, however, should be used with care because the performer may come to depend too heavily upon it and will not develop internal feedback. The type of feedback that should be given depends on the ability of the performer, the type of activity being undertaken and the personality of the performer – different performers respond differently to different types of feedback.

When performance is measured and is given to performers as feedback, their motivation can be enhanced and their performance improved. Negative feedback can be used effectively at times as a motivational tool and to encourage self-reflection. Sports performers often set themselves targets from their previous performances but teachers and coaches can help by constructing performance/goal charts that the performer updates as necessary. These charts serve as feedback on current performance and set clear and progressive targets.

Performance profiling and the observation analysis technique

As a coach when you analyse an individual's or a team's performance, you may wish to use some form of performance analysis. This includes observation and possibly the use of a video recorder. (Make sure you get permission to do this and ensure that you fulfil the requirements of the Child Protection Act.)

 **ACTIVITY 1**

TASK

Write a briefing paper designed for a coach or instructor to show the importance of feedback and the right sort of feedback to motivate the participant and to ensure that they learn effectively.

MOTIVATION

Motivation
A need or drive to do something with determination; for example, to go to a regular fitness class, to do more walking, to keep turning up to hockey practice in the hope of getting picked for the next game, to try hard to win in a game of football because you want to feel that you have done your best.

It is important for participants in physical activities, for those who want to follow a healthy lifestyle and for sports performers to be well motivated, but some seem to be better motivated than others. Some decide to be physically active for only a short period of time, whereas some seem addicted to exercise. When two athletes of very similar ability race against each other the winner is invariably the one who is better motivated.

There are some people who do not seem at all interested in participating in physical activities or, indeed, in following a healthy lifestyle. It is important to find out what actually motivates people to participate, follow a healthy lifestyle and do well in sport because we can then encourage more people to be fit and healthy and also to be involved in sport and performing at a higher level.

PRACTICAL APPLICATIONS

An athlete may be driven to achieve a personal best in throwing the discus. She is driven by the strong desire for self-fulfilment – to feel that she has challenged herself and has won.

A working dad feels motivated to go to the local leisure centre and join a five-a-side league because he feels he should be fitter to look after his family.

Fig 2.11 People may take up sport for all sorts of reasons

Intrinsic motivation
This is an inner drive or need to do well and succeed and to feel good and enjoy the activity.

Internal or intrinsic motivation

Intrinsic motivation is the internal drive or willpower that people have to participate in physical activities or to perform well in sport. Intrinsic motives include fun, enjoyment and the satisfaction that is experienced by achieving something or simply in doing it for its own sake. Some athletes describe the intrinsic 'flow' experienced during competition. They speak of high levels of concentration and a feeling that they are in total control.

Fig 2.12 Age is no barrier to enjoying sport

 PRACTICAL APPLICATIONS

A club tennis player who is 50 years of age reports that when he plays he often feels a sense of relief from the day's stresses and strains and that he enjoys the hard physical work of playing tennis. This is an example of **intrinsic** motivation.

 **Extrinsic motivation**

This is the drive or need that is caused by motives that are external or environmental. These motives are rewards that can be tangible or intangible.

External or extrinsic motivation

Extrinsic motivation involves influences external to the performer; for instance, the drive to do well in physical activity or sport could come from the need to please others or to gain rewards like medals or badges – or in some cases large amounts of money. Rewards that include badges or prize money are referred to as *tangible rewards*. Rewards that involve getting first place in the league or getting praise from your parents are known as *intangible rewards*.

Extrinsic motivation is very useful in encouraging people to follow a healthy lifestyle and to participate and achieve a better performance in sport.

Extrinsic motivation can increase levels of intrinsic motivation. If, for example, you win the cup in boxing this will probably result in you feeling good about the activity and enjoying boxing in future bouts. If you get praise from your family for exercising after school you will feel good when exercising.

 PRACTICAL APPLICATIONS

A young girl is just starting to learn to swim. After much effort she achieves a width of the pool without any help and without armbands. She is given a badge, which clearly shows everyone else that she has achieved success. This reward is pleasurable to the girl and her interest and determination in swimming increases. The reward is an example of extrinsic motivation which has **reinforced** the correct behaviour.

Ego motivation and task motivation

Another way of describing intrinsic and extrinsic motivation is identifying those who exercise and also sports performers as having:

- ego orientation: exercising or playing sport because you want to win or want to beat others (mostly extrinsic)
- task orientation: exercising to keep healthy, or playing sport because you enjoy improving your own personal best performances (mostly intrinsic)

You can have both kinds of motivation – but it is best either to be high in both ego and task orientation or low in ego and high in task orientation. People with these types of motivation try hard to keep exercising and to follow a healthy lifestyle and do not give up when things are not going well.

People who are high in ego orientation and low in task orientation may give up when they are no longer winning or beating other people.

Motivation for different roles

The role of participant

You may be motivated to please others (extrinsic) or to enjoy yourself and forget about your worries (intrinsic). Some young people take up activities like skateboarding, for example. Most try it to see whether they enjoy it, while others may try it in order to fit in with their peers or because friends expect them to.

ACTIVITY 2

TASK

Write down the physical activities/sports you are involved in. Next to each write why you think you took up that activity and then why you are still doing it.

CHALLENGE

Write down three strategies that might encourage people of your age to take up exercise or a physical activity. Identify whether these are intrinsic or extrinsic motivating factors.

www.bbc.co.uk/sport
Take the link from here to the Sports Academy where there are examples/case studies of well-motivated sports participants.

www.brianmac.co.uk
Has features on motivation/techniques for coaches.

www.sportsofficialsuk.com
The official website for sports officials has information related to motivation and the role of officials in sport.

The role of leader

You may want to take on a leadership role; for example, to run a lower school football or netball team. You may wish to lead an exercise class or to coach in a martial art. Whatever your leadership role, you may do it because you enjoy the feeling of encouraging others (intrinsic) or you may like the praise from others and the recognition that you are doing a good job (extrinsic).

The role of official

You might wish to umpire or referee a game of cricket or football or you may volunteer to be a basketball table official or a ball boy or girl at a tennis competition. Whichever official role you take there are many reasons why you might wish to do it. You might like the power it gives you and the fact that it makes you feel good; this is intrinsic motivation. It may be that you want to help others take up an activity and this gives you satisfaction – again intrinsic. You may be striving to achieve a coaching qualification to further your career (extrinsic) or because you don't want to let your teacher or coach down (also extrinsic).

GOAL SETTING

By setting goals you can:

- take up an activity or activities
- achieve more
- improve your performance
- improve your training
- increase your motivation
- increase your pride and satisfaction.

Goal setting is a very powerful technique that can lead to rewards and increase your motivation levels.

By knowing what you want to achieve, you know what you need to concentrate on and improve and what distractions to ignore.

PRACTICAL APPLICATIONS

When you set goals try to:
- pace yourself – do not try to do too much too soon
- give yourself rewards
- keep goals realistic
- keep a record of your goals
- avoid feeling bad if things don't go well – plan your next step.

Achieving goals

When you have achieved a goal, enjoy the satisfaction of having done it – pat yourself on the back. Plan to achieve even greater or higher goals.

If you have failed to reach a goal, make sure that you have learned lessons from it.

Reasons for not attaining your goals:

- you didn't try hard enough
- poor technique which needs to be adjusted
- the goals were unrealistic at this time.

Use this information to adjust your goals or to set different goals for learning new skills or improving your fitness. Turn everything into a positive learning experience. Failing to meet a goal is a step forward towards success.

When you have achieved a goal:

- if it was easily achieved, make your next goals harder
- if it took too long to achieve, make the next goals a little easier
- if you learned something that should lead you to change future goals, then change them.

Effective goal setting

For goal setting to be effective there must be short-term goals leading to medium-term goals and, eventually, to longer-term goals; for example, to win the league cup, the netball team may have to concentrate on winning more games away from home. For this to be achieved, there may be short-term goals of improving the defending strategies of the team. For those who simply wish to exercise more the first step is to walk to school rather than attempting any long-distance running.

Motivation can be increased by splitting long-term goals into stages according to how specific they are and what period of time they can be managed in.

SMARTER goal setting

Be able to identify each element and then apply it using a practical example; e.g. the specific goal of improving the serve technique in tennis.

S specific – if goals are clear and unambiguous they are more likely to be attained

M measurable – this is important for monitoring, and makes you accountable

A agreed – the sharing of goal setting between parents, personal trainer, coach and performer can give a sense of teamwork

R realistic – motivation will improve if goals can actually be reached

T timed – splitting your objectives up into short-term goals that are planned and progressive can be effective

E exciting – the more stimulating the activities are, the more motivating they will be

R recorded – a record is crucial for monitoring; once a goal is achieved it can be crossed off your list, thus improving motivation.

Stress management aids the performance of physical activities and is important to high-level performers as well as those at the other end of the spectrum who might be visiting the gym for the very first time. Goal setting is a useful strategy for controlling anxiety and one that is widely used in sport for training and performance.

Fig 2.13 Both beginner and elite athletes can benefit from the management of stress

Evaluation of goal setting

Goal evaluation must take place if progress is to be made and performance improved or participation increased. Goals must therefore be clearly defined. This is easier with physical activities and sports that involve objective measurements such as times. Evaluation can only take place if goals are measurable. The measurement of goals provides information about success, in itself a motivating factor, and also gives useful information about the setting of further goals.

Both those who exercise and sports performers need to know how they are progressing. Most sports people are highly motivated and feedback is essential for them to maintain their enthusiasm and commitment. For those who are exercising to keep fit positive feedback is again crucial in encouraging them to keep going – too many people who join gyms in the UK do not actually attend other than the first few times.

 **PRACTICAL APPLICATIONS**

There has been a sharp decline in the number of people joining gyms over the past five years. 54,000 fewer people took out gym membership in 2007 than in 2002.

For some people the gym has been pushed aside by yoga, pilates and outdoor boot-camp-style programmes such as 'military fitness circuits'.

At the time of writing almost a quarter of British adults are judged to be obese and, if current trends continue, 60 per cent of men and 50 per cent of women are likely to be clinically obese by 2050.

Yoga and pilates studios are on the increase, more people are running now than during the jogging boom of the 1980s, and participation in activities as varied as ballroom dancing, ice-skating and triathlons is rising. It has become obvious to consumers that there are other, more appealing, means of burning calories than going to the gym – and that even walking the dog or cycling to work can be good exercise.

If people exercise simply to lose weight, not because they enjoy it, they will either give up before they achieve their goal or will think 'job done' when their target weight is reached, then revert to their old habits of inactivity.

Many surveys have indicated that, six months after joining, the dropout rate among new gym members is about 60 per cent. One report suggested that 20 per cent of health-club members work out there no more than once a month.

ACTIVITY 3

TASK

Read the above 'practical applications' information. Summarise why you think that gym membership is dropping and why gyms have not been very successful in getting people fit.

CHALLENGE

Write a short essay suggesting ways in which you can encourage people to get fit other than going to a gym. What aspects of lifestyle could be changed at no extra cost?

REVIEW QUESTIONS

1 What is meant by fundamental motor skills?
2 Which are the main fundamental motor skills?
3 How can you describe each fundamental motor skill?
4 In what ways can you analyse each fundamental motor skill?
5 How do we learn motor skills by practising?
6 Why do we copy some people and not others?
7 What do we need to take into consideration if we want someone to copy a demonstration of a motor skill?
8 What is meant by trial and error learning?
9 What are role models?
10 How can feedback help in the learning of motor skills?
11 What is the difference between knowledge of performance and knowledge of results?
12 What is meant by motivation?
13 What are the differences between intrinsic and extrinsic motivation?
14 What might motivate you to participate, lead and become an official?
15 Why is goal setting important?
16 What makes goal setting more effective?

EXAM-STYLE QUESTIONS

Multiple choice questions

1 Feedback on performance is especially important because:
   a It gives the performer information about the result of the activity.
   b It increases competition.
   c It helps to control anxiety.
   d It helps to improve technique.

2 We are more likely to copy a role model for the following reasons except:
   a We relate to them.
   b They are good at what they do.
   c They are our friend.
   d They are attractive to us.

3 What is the main reason for SMART goal setting?
   a To punish those who do not stick to their exercise programme.
   b To reward financially if you stick to the exercise programme.
   c To check whether the coach is doing a good job.
   d To motivate participants to follow an exercise programme.

4 Which one of the following is an example of extrinsic motivation?
   a Trying to beat your personal best in a 100 metre sprint.
   b Participating in badminton for enjoyment.
   c Wanting to swim a length of the swimming baths to gain a badge.
   d Taking up aerobics to get fitter.

Short answer questions

1 Identify two fundamental motor skills that would be part of the long jump. **(2 marks)**
2 Explain how skills in physical activities can be learned effectively. **(4 marks)**
3 Describe four different types of feedback. **(4 marks)**
4 Describe ways in which we might assess the motor skill learning of others. **(4 marks)**
5 Explain how you would analyse the performance of the fundamental motor skills of running and throwing. **(4 marks)**
6 Explain how goal setting can help to improve performance in a physical activity. **(4 marks)**
7 Identify and explain three extrinsic motivating factors that are important for a performer learning new skills. **(6 marks)**

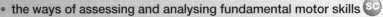 **WHAT YOU NEED TO KNOW**

- what is meant by fundamental movement skills, and some practical examples

- the ways of assessing and analysing fundamental motor skills (SC)

- methods of learning skills

- different types of feedback in learning skills

- how feedback helps to motivate participants in physical activities

- definitions of intrinsic and extrinsic motivation with examples (SC)

- how motivation relates to the different roles of participant, leader and official (SC)

- the importance of goal setting in performance and participation and in controlling anxiety (SC)

- the SMART principle of goal setting.

CHAPTER 3

DECISION MAKING IN DIFFERENT ROLES

LEARNING GOALS

By the end of this chapter you should be able to:

* identify and describe the roles of participant, leader and official in a number of different physical activities

* identify and describe the different types of decision making in physical activities SC

* explain the importance of abiding by rules and codes of behaviour in physical activities SC

* explain the importance of etiquette and sportsmanship. SC

THE ROLES AND DECISIONS OF PARTICIPANTS, LEADERS AND OFFICIALS

There are a number of different roles you can choose if you wish to be involved in physical activities. Young people now have a wide range of opportunities for involvement. You can follow an active, healthy lifestyle in a variety of ways. Simply participating in playing a sport or exercising are not the only ways of being actively involved. As a leader, teacher or coach or as an official of some sort you can still get high levels of physical and mental activity and interest.

 Role
The part played by someone in a particular situation, e.g. as a player in a rugby team or as a member of a yoga class. The part played is influenced by the expectations of others about what is appropriate; for example, in an exercise class you are expected to follow instructions and to work hard and possibly help others.

 ACTIVITY 1

TASK
List as many ways as possible in which you can participate in physical activities in your school or college; for example, as a netball player, an athlete, a member of a circuit training club, etc.
   Make a list of other possible physical activities that could be run in your school and college – but be realistic!

CHALLENGE
Evaluate why so few young people want to take up the role of an official in physical activities. How would you make such a role attractive to young people?

Fig 3.1 The role you play in physical activities is influenced by the expectations of others

The role of participant

As a participant in a physical activity (for example, an exercise class or your chosen sport) you will play a role. That role might be to follow the instructions from the class tutor, or in a sport it might be to score as many goals as possible or to be the captain.

 ACTIVITY 2

TASK
As a participant in your chosen physical activity make a list of your responsibilities or the ways in which you are expected to behave. These responsibilities make up your role in that activity.

CHALLENGE
Choose a role in exercise or sport and compare it with another role in a different sport or physical activity.

The role of leader

There are many different ways you can lead in a physical activity. You can follow the role of a coach or an instructor or you could be captain of the team. You could be responsible for teaching a group, or assisting teaching a group, in physical activities.

There are many skills associated with being a good coach or leader of a sports activity. The skill of communicating with performers and other coaches, as well as officials, is very important if the leader is going to get the best out of everyone. Communication can be verbal and non-verbal, and effective communication does include listening.

 PRACTICAL APPLICATIONS

Communication skills of the sports leader should include the ability to:

- be direct – make instructions brief and easy to understand
- be consistent – avoid double meanings, contradictions and confusion
- separate fact from opinion – be accurate in your analysis rather than giving an emotional response
- focus on one thing at a time – too much information causes information overload
- repeat key points – this reinforces the message and avoids misunderstandings
- have a good 'sense of audience' – adapt your content and technique depending on the recipient.

Good communication in leading a sports activity should also include the following practical aspects:

- Talk to individuals as they train or exercise. Make sure they know that you know them.
- Use positive comments rather than negative ones if at all possible, but don't give praise unless it is deserved.
- Ensure that you can control a group of young people by insisting that they respond to a signal; for example, a whistle – stress the health and safety aspect of this.
- Use your voice and vary your tone. Shout if necessary but not too often – bring the group up to you to give instructions rather than shouting.
- Use questions to try to find out what the group members know and understand.

Try to make sessions fun so that motivation is high – and do not pick on individuals and embarrass them.

An effective leader or coach would be one who is well organised. Good organisation can relieve possible sources of stress and can ultimately help performance. Confidence in the leader or coach is increased if the performer perceives him or herself to be organised. Self-confidence on the part of the leader or coach can also be increased if personal organisation is good.

 PRACTICAL APPLICATIONS

To be well organised make sure that you:

- plan well in advance and make the necessary arrangements for the activity to go smoothly
- prepare and organise the facilities that you will use
- prepare the equipment and check it for safety as well as for appropriateness; e.g., is there enough equipment for everyone to use?
- work well with others who are sharing the leadership and develop a sense of teamwork – do you each know what the other is doing?
- plan your session to take into account time, available facilities and the ability of the learners
- can change your plans if things do not go well or circumstances change; for example, have you made a plan if the weather is wet and you are outside?

The skills of analysing and problem solving are also important for effective leading or coaching. You need to be able to analyse what exactly is going wrong, then it is more likely that the problem will be solved. Analysis might reveal problems with the skills that the learners are performing, with their behaviour or with the suitability of the activity.

Leaders or coaches also need to have skills in educating learners regarding the following:

- **hydration** – types of hydration, reasons for hydration, hydration recommendations before, during and after exercise
- **sports psychology** – including: basic goal-setting principles (definitions of goal setting and SMART-type goal setting); basic motivational principles (what motivates people to exercise and the difference in motivating children and adults)
- **physiology** – including the principles of warm-up and cool-down; fitness components, strength, speed, flexibility, power, agility and muscular endurance; the basic principles of strength, speed, power and endurance training; the principles of training – overload, progression, specificity, adaptation, variability, reversibility, recovery and over-training.

The qualities of a good leader include using good communication skills with other leaders and the participants. A good leader is enthusiastic and well motivated themselves. It is easier to enthuse others if you seem to be enjoying your job as leader! Having good exercise and sports skills yourself helps, particularly for demonstrations, but is not essential. If you have a good in-depth knowledge of the activity or sport then it is easier to gain respect. The standard of appearance is also important, especially with young people. If you want the group members to be suitably 'kitted out' for the activity then it is important that you too 'look the part' and are smartly and appropriately dressed. You must always be **punctual** and **reliable.** If you wish your participants to turn up on time and to attend regularly, then you must set a good example for them to follow.

A good leader is often charismatic – in other words, he or she naturally commands respect because of their personality. A good leader will have a clear vision of what they are trying to achieve and so good planning and organisation is essential if you are to be a successful leader in a sports activity.

 ACTIVITY 3

TASK

Choose a role of leader in a physical activity – this might be as captain of a sports team, coach of a lower-school sports team or leader of an aerobics class. List what makes the role of leader effective so that you can give advice to others who may wish to take up the role.

CHALLENGE

Watch a leader in a physical activity – a coach or an instructor, for example. Make a note of what he or she does successfully and what could be improved. Write a short critique of the session.

The role of official

Being an official may mean refereeing a game or judging a gymnastics competition. It could also mean that you help to organise a competition or physical activity. Other roles of officials include umpires, scorers, timekeepers, table officials, lines persons and starters.

 PRACTICAL APPLICATIONS

FOOTBALL OFFICIAL

It is often said that the men and women who are referees are having a good game if you don't notice them.

The referee, with a whistle, takes charge of a match, with the help of two assistant referees. In professional matches, a fourth official is also involved. The referee enforces the laws of the game, awarding free kicks if there is any foul play and keeping a check on the time. The 'ref' can also postpone, stop, suspend or call off a match if there are weather or crowd problems. The assistant referee helps out with decisions such as throw-ins and offsides and sometimes will have a better view of incidents than the referee. The fourth official is based on the touchline, assisting with substitutions and keeping a check on the managers.

Officials' responsibilities

The long list of officials' responsibilities includes appearance, personal equipment, fitness, knowledge and use of rules and regulations, control of game, safety of players/individuals, playing equipment, playing surfaces, fair play and spirit of the game.

Communication

Aspects of officials' communication skills include use of voice, confidence, use of whistle, hand signals, decision making, interpretation of rules, terminology, scoring, starting and judging.

Judgement

The basic role of the official can described as being 'safe' and 'fair'. By viewing the game with these two words in mind, an official should be able to officiate in a way that is acceptable to all of the participants.

The word 'fair' does allow some flexibility in determining which infractions will and will not be penalised. Remember that it is the 'spirit' or 'intent' of the rule that determines an infraction. This will be interpreted differently in each game, depending on the official, the level of play and the style of play. As officials develop their officiating skills, their 'feel for the game' and judgement will help them determine the officiating style needed in each game.

There is no excuse for an official not to penalise any infraction that threatens the safety of another participant.

www.englandnetball.co.uk
Has information on rules and regulations for netball.

www.englandbasketball.co.uk
Go to this site for up-to-date rules and codes of conduct.

 PRACTICAL APPLICATIONS

BASKETBALL OFFICIALS
On the scorers' table, there are table officials, who are responsible for the administration of the game. The table officials include the scorer, who keeps track of the score, time outs and fouls by each player; the timer, who controls the scoreboard; and the stop-clock operator.

Fig 3.2 Often, officials have to make difficult judgements on the spot

Referees and umpires generally wear different coloured kit/uniform. These officials are responsible for the overall management of the game, to ensure the teams compete in a fair, honest and consistent environment.

Records of officials in physical contests go back to Ancient Greece and other early civilisations. During the ancient Olympics they appointed *Hellanodikai* (officials) who lived in seclusion for ten months prior to the games and prepared to officiate the games. The *Hellanodikai*'s decisions were final and athletes as well as their coaches faced harsh punishment for not following the rules.

Effective and fair officiating is often no less demanding a role than playing or coaching the game. The sports official's role is unique as it requires a familiarity with the game, the athletes, coaches and spectators and at the same time it demands an emotional distance from an often highly charged environment.

PRACTICAL APPLICATIONS

GUIDELINES FOR AN OFFICIAL
- Officials should be firm, but not arrogant; fair, but not officious.
- Officials should try to understand the behaviour of the participants.
- Officials should referee or umpire and give judgements regardless of pressure from fans, the score, whom it will hurt, or how it will affect their future relations with coaches and athletes.
- The official's reputation should be built on honesty and integrity.
- Officials should be role models if they are to be respected by the players, coaches and spectators.

RULES, REGULATIONS AND CODES OF BEHAVIOUR IN PHYSICAL ACTIVITY AND SPORT

Rules and regulations are designed to protect individuals who participate, lead or officiate in physical activity and sport. If the laws, regulations and guidelines are followed properly and checked thoroughly there is much less likelihood of an accident happening and people's lives being put at risk. Rules also allow the activity to be played fairly and include boundaries of behaviour involving mutual respect and the protection of all participants' well-being.

Rules
These are usually set by National Governing Bodies for team, racket and individual sports. Other physical activities have their own rules relating to healthy and safety and fair practice.

Regulations
These are specifications relating to players and participants, umpires/referees, timekeepers, lines persons, starters and judges, equipment, playing surfaces, facilities and safe practice.

Scoring systems
These involve methods of determining who has won, and methods of scoring in specific team, racket and individual sports and physical activities where appropriate.

Fig 3.3 A detailed breakdown of the score after the match can help a player to improve in future matches, but really it is the final result that counts

 Etiquette
This is about codes of behaviour, the customs surrounding the rules and regulations of a physical activity and also about what is socially acceptable in a particular culture. It involves a convention or an accepted way of behaving in a particular situation. In sport this is often viewed as sportsmanship.

If rules are broken then in most physical activities there are consequences. In some sports these are penalties, such as losing territory or being sent off, and in other activities it may involve being fined or even taken to court.

Rules are often made to protect participants – for example, to prevent unreasonable demands being made on young people.

PRACTICAL APPLICATIONS

In the 2008 Beijing Olympics alleged discrepancies came to light about the age of He Kexin, the host nation's gymnast who won gold in both team and individual events. An official inquiry was launched that could result in the gymnast being stripped of her medals. Some think they have evidence to show that she was 14 rather than 16 – the minimum age limit for the Olympics.

Fig 3.4 Rules are often made to protect young participants

PRACTICAL APPLICATIONS

THE ETIQUETTE IN CRICKET
Cricket has always been seen as the gentleman's game – and that means there are certain traditions of the game that should be respected. Here are some examples of good cricketing etiquette:

WALK WHEN YOU'RE OUT
Sadly this is a tradition that has gone out of the game at the highest level. But there will be times when a batsman has been caught out by the wicket keeper, but this is missed by the umpire; whether you own up to being out and walk back to the pavilion is your decision but it is regarded as good etiquette to do so.

UMPIRE'S DECISION IS FINAL
Once a decision has been made, there's no turning back. So that means no arguing with the umpire.

APPLAUD THE NEW BATSMAN
No matter whether you're playing for your school or your country, it's good etiquette to clap the new batsman making their way to the wicket.

Good etiquette or sportsmanship involve fairness and generosity. Those who show good sportsmanship (and this includes women, in spite of the term!) stick to the rules and regulations but also show that they can lose gracefully and with good humour.

If you compete in a physical activity it is often good to shake your opponent's hand before and after the event. If you accidentally hurt or injure an opponent you would show good sportsmanship by showing more concern for the well-being of that person than for winning the game.

In exercise generally there are good manners in using facilities and equipment; for example, if you are working out in a gymnasium you return the free weights back to the containing rack after you have used them. If you use exercise equipment then it is good manners to towel it down afterwards to remove your sweat.

Fig 3.5 Good sportsmanship makes for a pleasant and respectful environment

ACTIVITY 4

TASK
Make a list of the main rules for participating in your favourite physical activity.

CHALLENGE
Choose a physical activity and then write a set of etiquette guidelines for that activity. Don't write about the actual rules but state what is acceptable and what is not as far as behaviour is concerned.

Examples of good sportsmanship or etiquette:

- Shake hands with your opponent.
- Thank anyone who has been participating with you or against you.
- Show concern for others, especially when they are injured or under stress.
- Never swear or be abusive.
- Do not stretch the rules to gain an advantage over someone else.
- Take defeat well and show good humour.
- Do not question officials – accept their decisions.
- Say 'well done' to opponents when they do well.
- Take other people into consideration when participating in exercise – for example, avoid colliding with others when swimming.
- Do not over-celebrate when you do well – take other people's feelings into account and avoid arrogance in victory.
- Do not deride the efforts of others – be respectful whatever their ability.

REVIEW QUESTIONS

1 What is meant by a role?
2 What roles are there in physical activities?
3 What are the characteristics of the role of an official?
4 What is the role of a leader in physical activities?
5 What decisions have to be made in each role?
6 What is meant by etiquette when applied to physical activities?
7 Give some examples of good etiquette in a range of physical activities.

 EXAM-STYLE QUESTIONS

Multiple choice questions

1 Which one of the following is not an active role in physical activity?
  a an umpire
  b a referee
  c a spectator
  d a coach
2 The role of an official is primarily which of the following?
  a fair but firm
  b strict but friendly
  c to keep to time
  d to make money
3 It is recognised that physical activities should be conducted according to appropriate codes of behaviour or etiquette. Which of the following is not an example of good etiquette when performing a physical activity?
  a shaking hands with your opponent at the end of a tennis match
  b obeying the referee in football.
  c shouting 'well played' to one of your teammates in hockey
  d politely questioning a decision made by the referee in basketball

Short answer questions

1 In an activity of your choice describe how good sportsmanship might be displayed by a participant.   **(3 marks)**
2 Describe the different types of roles associated with physical activities.   **(3 marks)**
3 Give examples of different types of decision making as a performer in a physical activity.   **(3 marks)**

 WHAT YOU NEED TO KNOW

- the role of participant in a number of different physical activities and the decisions they have to make (SC)
- the role of leader in a number of different physical activities and the decisions they have to make (SC)
- the role of an official in a number of different physical activities and the decisions they have to make (SC)
- the importance of abiding by rules and codes of behaviour in physical activities.
- the importance of etiquette and sportsmanship. (SC)

4.1 COMPONENTS OF FITNESS

LEARNING GOALS

By the end of this section, you should be able to:
- identify the health-related components of fitness (SC)
- describe these components (SC)
- explain how an active, healthy and balanced lifestyle affects each component (SC)
- explain the importance of the 'warm-up' and 'cool-down', with practical examples. (SC)

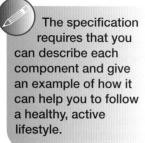
The specification requires that you can describe each component and give an example of how it can help you to follow a healthy, active lifestyle.

Haemoglobin
This is found in the blood and is an iron-rich protein. Haemoglobin transports or carries oxygen in the blood. Endurance-type exercise can increase the amount of haemoglobin and therefore increase the amount of oxygen available for us to use.

HEALTH-RELATED COMPONENTS OF FITNESS

If we follow a healthy, balanced lifestyle then our overall health and fitness will benefit. The health-related components of fitness all affect our ability to exercise and to follow an active, healthy and balanced lifestyle.

Cardiovascular endurance or stamina

The cardiovascular system involves transporting oxygen around the body. The cardiovascular system includes:

- the heart
- the network of blood vessels
- the blood.

The benefits of a healthy, balanced lifestyle for the cardiovascular system include:

- healthy capillaries and, through exercise, an increase in capillary density and efficiency
- a healthy heart that is less likely to suffer from heart disease and eventually, through exercise, a lower resting heart rate
- good blood circulation; with exercise this can increase the amount of blood pumped by the heart both at rest and during exercise
- healthy blood pressure and, with exercise, a decrease in resting blood pressure
- feeling energetic because of the uptake of oxygen by the body; with exercise there may be an increase in **haemoglobin**, which helps carry oxygen, along with an increase in red blood cells
- feeling less tired both physically and mentally.

✓ **Slow-twitch fibres (sometimes called Type 1 muscle fibres)**
These are muscle fibres that can produce energy over a long period of time. They have high levels of myoglobin and mitochondria and are used mainly for aerobic activities.

Mitochondria
These are places in each muscle cell where energy is produced – sometimes referred to as the 'powerhouses' of muscle cells. Those who exercise regularly and participate in endurance activities such as long-distance cycling often have more mitochondria.

Myoglobin
This is a type of haemoglobin found in muscle cells that transport oxygen to the mitochondria to produce energy. Those who are more active – especially those who exercise regularly for endurance events such as marathon running – have higher levels of myoglobin.

⚽ **PRACTICAL APPLICATIONS**

Exercise may help improve mental performance in adults. A University of Melbourne team tested the impact of a home-based physical-activity programme on 138 volunteers aged 50 and over with memory problems. Those who took part showed a modest improvement in cognitive function compared to those who did not.

A *Journal of the American Medical Association* study suggests exercise may help ward off severe mental decline. Dementia is already a serious problem, and the number of people with Alzheimer's disease, the most common form of the condition, is predicted to quadruple worldwide over the next half century. The latest study focused on people with mild cognitive impairment, a term used to describe memory problems that are not serious enough to interfere with everyday life. It does not necessarily lead to dementia, but does increase risk of developing the condition.

Some volunteers were asked to complete three 50-minute sessions a week of moderate physical activity, such as walking, for 24 weeks. Others were not asked to increase their exercise levels. At the end of the study, the people in the exercise group achieved better scores in tests of their cognitive function, and lower scores in tests to determine signs of dementia. Follow-up showed that the benefits persisted for at least another 12 months after the exercise programme was stopped.

Exercise is known to help keep the cardiovascular system healthy, and may help boost cognitive function by boosting blood supply to the brain.

Source: *Journal of the American Medical Association* September 3, 2008 300:1027–1037

Muscular endurance

This is the ability of the muscle or group of muscles to repeatedly contract or keep going without rest.

With a healthy, balanced lifestyle the muscles can keep going longer because of greater **aerobic** potential. Activities like swimming or running can enlarge **slow-twitch** fibres, enhancing potential for energy production. Onset of fatigue is delayed because of higher maximum oxygen uptake (VO_2max.) Muscles are also healthier and, through exercise, the size and number of **mitochondria** are increased.

With exercise there is also an increase in **myoglobin** content within the muscle cell.

There are also **anaerobic** adaptations in the muscles after exercise. Activities like sprinting or weight lifting can cause the increase in size of the fast-twitch muscle fibres (**hypertrophy**).

The heart muscle becomes healthier and after exercise the size of the heart can increase – this is called cardiac hypertrophy.

Fig 4.1.1 Muscular endurance is the ability of the muscle or group of muscles to repeatedly contract or keep going without rest

Fig 4.1.2 Marathon runners have higher levels of myoglobin

Speed

This is the ability of the body to move quickly. The movements may be the whole body or parts of the body; for example, arm speed in cricket bowling. As part of a healthy lifestyle it is often important to be able to move quickly; for example, when running for a bus.

Fig 4.1.3 As part of a healthy lifestyle it is often important to be able to move quickly (for example, when running for a bus)

With a healthy, balanced lifestyle your speed is affected because:

• your heart and lungs are more efficient
• your muscles can move quicker because they have more energy available
• more energy is available because your muscles are more efficient in producing energy
• your joints are healthier and move more freely.

Strength

This is the ability of the muscular system to exert force for a short period of time. The amount of force that can be exerted depends on the size, number and co-ordination of the muscles involved, as well as the type of muscle fibres used. As part of a healthy lifestyle it is important to have sufficient strength to lift and carry objects. Strength is also an asset in many sports; for example, when hitting a ball hard in tennis.

With a healthy balanced lifestyle your strength is improved because:

- an active lifestyle that includes exercise like cycling can enlarge **slow-twitch fibres**, which gives greater potential for energy production
- the size and number of mitochondria is increased, as is the myoglobin content in the muscle cells
- there are anaerobic benefits to muscles, with activities like sprinting causing the muscle to get bigger and stronger (**hypertrophy).**

Flexibility

This is the amount or range of movement that you can have around a joint. The structure of the joint restricts movement as well as the muscles, tendons and ligaments (more about these later in this part). As part of a healthy lifestyle it is important to have flexibility or suppleness to prevent strains and move faster and more effectively. If we are flexible then when we exercise and go about our daily activities we are less likely to be injured or experience stresses and strains to our muscles and joints.

✓ **Hypertrophy**
This term means that there is an increase in the size or the mass of an organ in the body or a muscle. Hypertrophy often occurs as a result of regular training or exercise.

Fig 4.1.4 As part of a healthy lifestyle it is important to have flexibility or suppleness to prevent strains and move faster and more effectively

A healthy, balanced lifestyle improves your flexibility because:

- your ligaments and supporting tissues can stretch further
- the blood flow to your muscles is improved
- the rise in muscle temperature can help muscles to be more flexible
- the more the body is used to stretching, the more able it is to stretch further.

Many of us strive, to a greater or lesser degree, for a healthy lifestyle that will enable us to carry out the physical and mental demands of everyday life and perhaps also to be involved in leisure or sports activities.

Fig 4.1.5 We need to be fit and healthy in order to lead active, productive everyday lives

We need to be fit and healthy to enable us to:

● work for a living or go to school/college
● look after other members of our families and our friends
● physically move from one place to another; for example, walk to school without getting out of breath
● play sports and engage in leisure activities
● make friends and socialise
● avoid illness and injury
● feel good in ourselves
● have a good sense of self-esteem or self-worth.

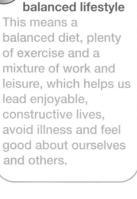

Healthy, balanced lifestyle
This means a balanced diet, plenty of exercise and a mixture of work and leisure, which helps us lead enjoyable, constructive lives, avoid illness and feel good about ourselves and others.

Fig 4.1.6 A fit and healthy lifestyle can help us to have high self-esteem

Make sure that you know what a fit, healthy and balanced lifestyle means, with some practical examples not just in sport but in everyday life.

ACTIVITY 1

TASK
List the main activities/tasks that you have undertaken over the past three days that require you to be fit and healthy. Are there any areas of your health/fitness that need improving?

CHALLENGE
Next to the list above write the types of health and fitness components that are used to carry out these activities.

THE WARM-UP AND COOL-DOWN ⓢⓒ

The warm-up and cool-down are very important aspects of any exercise and training programme.

The warm-up enables the body to prepare for the onset of exercise. It decreases the likelihood of injury and muscle soreness. There is also a release of adrenaline that will start the process of speeding up the delivery of oxygen to the working muscles. An increase in muscle temperature will help to ensure that there is a ready supply of energy and that the muscle becomes more flexible to prevent injury. Many also believe that the warm-up improves the speed and strength of muscle contractions.

Hold each warm-up stretch for a minimum of 20–30 seconds, breathing slowly through your nose, aiming to exhale out through your mouth as you ease into the stretch.

Fig 4.1.7 The warm-up enables the body to prepare for the onset of exercise

For best results, push against a wall.

Easy: Calf (correct foot position)

Foot alignment should be shoulder width apart. You can confirm this by standing either side of a straight line on the floor.

When you take your rear foot back, it should not cross or move away from the midline, your foot should be pointing forward with your heel either flat on the floor, or raised if aiming to develop the stretch.

Your front leg should bend so that when you look down over your knee, you can see the tip of your toes. Lean forward aiming to keep a straight line with your heel, hip and head.

Easy: Soleus

1 Stand with both feet flat on the floor, pointing forward, half a stride apart.

2 Keeping your back straight, with your hands on your hips, exhale and lower yourself down, resting your bodyweight on the rear foot.

Easy: Normal stretch

1 Stand with your feet shoulder-width apart, one foot extended half a step forward.

2 Keeping the front leg straight, bend your rear leg, resting both hands on the bent thigh.

3 Slowly exhale, aiming to tilt both buttocks upward, keeping the front leg straight, and both feet flat on the floor, pointing forward.

4 Inhale slowly, and relax from this stretching exercise. Repeat the stretch again, this time beginning with the toes of the front foot raised toward the ceiling, but keeping the heel on the floor.

Easy: Quadriceps standing

1 Stand holding on to a secure object, or have one hand raised out to the side for balance.

2 Raise one heel up toward your buttocks, and grasp hold of your foot with one hand.

3 Inhale, slowly pulling your heel to your buttock while gradually pushing your pelvis forward.

4 Aim to keep both knees together, having a slight bend in the supporting leg.

Moderate: Leg over

1 Lie on your back, extending your left arm out to the side, while taking your left leg over your right, bringing the knee in line with the hips.

2 Keeping your right leg straight, use your right arm to push down on the knee of the left leg, exhaling slowly as you stretch.

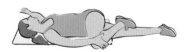

Easy: Foetal position

1 Lie on your back, keeping your head on the floor.

2 Slowly pull both legs into your chest, and secure them there by wrapping your arms around the back of your knees.

3 Exhale, pulling down on your legs while gradually lifting your buttocks off the floor.

4 You can stretch your neck, once in this position, by slowly tilting your chin to your chest.

Easy: Spine curve

1 Begin the stretch by lying on your front, with your hands close to your chest, fingers pointing upward.

2 Exhale, pushing yourself up with your arms and contracting your buttocks while keeping both feet firmly on the floor.

3 Look up toward the ceiling, to also feel the stretch in your neck.

Easy: Bar twist

1 Stand with both feet facing forward, double shoulder-width apart, with legs slightly bent.

2 Use the bar to keep your upper body straight, with elbows high, as you slowly twist around in both directions.

3 Avoid moving at speed or forcing the stretch.

Easy: Lower back (cat stretch)

1 Adopt a position on all fours, point your fingers forward and your toes behind.

2 Start with a flat back, and then drop your head downward, pushing your shoulder blades upward and outward as you elevate your upper back.

Easy: Elbows back

1 Stand or sit upright, keeping your back straight, head looking forward.

2 Place both hands on your lower back, fingers pointing downward, elbows out to your side.

3 Exhale slowly while gently pulling the elbows back, aiming to get them to touch.

Easy: Shoulder strangle

1 Cross one arm horizontally over your chest, grasping it with either your hand or forearm, just above the elbow joint.

2 Exhale, slowly pulling your upper arm in toward your chest.

3 Aim to keep the hips and shoulders facing forward throughout the stretch.

Easy: Bicep wall stretch

1 Place the palm, inner elbow, and shoulder of one arm against the wall.

2 Keeping the arm in contact with the wall, exhale and slowly turn your body around, to feel the stretch in your biceps and chest.

3 Adjust the hand position either higher or lower and repeat to stretch the multiple biceps and chest muscles.

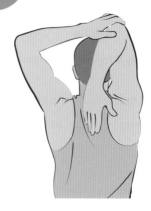

Easy-moderate: Hand down spine

1 Extend one hand down the centre of your back, fingers pointing downward.

2 Use the other hand to grasp the elbow.

3 Exhale slowly, pulling gently downward on your elbow, aiming to take your fingers along your spine.

Easy: Upward stretch

1 Extend both hands straight above your head, palms touching.

2 Inhale, slowly pushing your hands upward, then backward, keeping your back straight.

3 Exhale and relax from the stretch before you repeat.

Easy: Chin to chest front

1 Place both hands at the rear of your head, fingers interlocked, thumbs pointing down, elbows pointing straight ahead.

2 Slowly exhale, pulling your head downward, aiming for your chin to touch your chest.

3 Concentrate on keeping your back straight, with your shoulders down and back.

4 Relax your hands, and inhale as you lift your head.

The cool-down is important because if light exercise follows hard training, the oxygen can more effectively be flushed through the muscle tissue and oxidise lactic acid (there is more about the effects of lactic acid on p.64). Cool-downs also prevent blood pooling in the veins, which can cause dizziness. The cool-down speeds up the removal of lactic acid and other waste products. Many believe that a cool-down also prevents future stiffness and soreness and any resulting injuries.

Once you have finished any form of physical activity, you should gradually allow your heart rate and breathing to lower to a comfortable level where you can talk without getting breathless. Light aerobic exercise such as walking or easy indoor cycling are good, as both of these will allow you to hydrate yourself. Also you should put on warm clothing.

Hold each cool-down stretch for a minimum of 20–30 seconds, breathe comfortably, with deep breaths in through your nose and out via your mouth.

Easy: Calf raise down

1 Stand on a raised platform, on the balls of your feet, holding on to a secure object for balance.

2 Exhale, slowly dropping your heels down towards the floor and allowing your toes to raise naturally.

This movement can be performed using either one or both feet.

www.netfit.co.uk
For a range of exercises for warm-up and cool-down.

www.teachingideas.co.uk/pe
Has warm-up and cool-down with a list of appropriate activities.

Easy: Lying straight, leg to chest

1 Lie comfortably on your back, concentrating on keeping both your head and buttocks in contact with the floor.

2 Slowly extend one leg upward, grasping it with both hands, either around the calf, the hamstrings, or a combination of both.

3 Aim to pull your leg toward your chest, keeping it straight. When the tension builds up in your hamstrings, relax the stretch a little by contracting your quadriceps on the same leg.

4 If necessary, use a towel wrapped around your foot, in order to keep your head on the floor.

Easy: Stretch lying

1 Lie on your side, aiming to keep both the knees and the inside of your thighs together.

2 Extend the lower leg out straight, keeping the top leg bent, and one hand grasping the foot.

3 Exhale, pulling the foot toward your buttock while you slowly push your pelvis forward.

4 Use a towel wrapped around your foot if you can't reach your foot comfortably.

Easy: Toe grab

1 Begin this stretch with your heels together, holding both feet with your hands.

2 Lean forward from your hips, gradually increasing the stretch by bringing your heels closer to your groin and your chest closer to your feet.

3 Make the movements small and controlled. Avoid bouncing and excessive upward pressure on your feet.

Moderate: One leg over

1 Sit on the floor, with one leg straight, toes pointing upward.

2 Cross the other foot over the knee of the straight leg, aiming to place that foot flat on the floor.

3 Place the elbow and forearm of the opposite arm of the bent leg on the outside of the bent knee.

4 Exhale, slowly pulling the bent knee across your body.

Moderate: Looking at ceiling

1 Begin the stretch by kneeling on the floor, holding your heels with both hands.

2 Slowly exhale, lifting your buttocks up and forward while taking the head backward, in order to arch the back.

Easy-Moderate: Lying trunk twists

1 Lie flat on your back, with both hands extended straight out to your sides.

2 Slide both legs up towards one arm, aiming to keep the knees together, whilst allowing your lower body to naturally twist around.

3 Can be performed with either bent or straight legs.

Easy: Upper back leg grab

1 While seated, exhale, bending forward, and hugging your thighs underneath with both arms.

2 Keep your feet extended out as you pull your chest down on to your thighs, keeping both knees together.

3 While in this position, you can also stretch your rhomboids, by aiming to pull your upper back away from you knees while still grasping your legs.

Moderate: One arm against the wall

1 Place your forearm and biceps against a wall, keeping the arm at right angles.

2 Exhale, slowly turning your opposite shoulder backward, keeping the other arm firmly in contact with the wall.

3 Repeat this stretch both raising and lowering the walled arm, in order to work the different pectoral muscles (see p. 60).

Moderate: Upper back prayer

1 From a kneeling position, extend both hands out, fingers pointing forward.

2 Use your hands and forearms to grip the floor, as you gently ease your buttocks backward, until you feel the stretch in your upper back and shoulders.

3 Exhale, gently easing your chest down toward the floor.

Easy: Bicep wall stretch

1 Place the palm, inner elbow, and shoulder of one arm against the wall.

2 Keeping the arm in contact with the wall, exhale and slowly turn your body around, to feel the stretch in your biceps and pectoral muscles.

3 Adjust the hand position either higher or lower and repeat to stretch the multiple biceps and chest muscles.

Easy-Moderate: Hand down spine

1 Extend one hand down the centre of your back, fingers pointing downward.

2 Use the other hand to grasp the elbow.

3 Exhale slowly, pulling gently downward on your elbow, aiming to take your fingers along your spine.

Easy: Hands interlocked over head

1 Interlock your fingers above your head, palms facing upward.

2 Exhale and push your hands further above your head.

3 You will also feel this stretch in your shoulders.

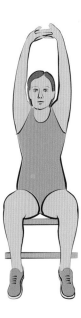

Easy-Moderate: Lying neck pull

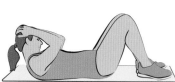

1 Lie on your back, with both legs bent, feet firmly flat on the floor.

2 Grasp the back of your head with your fingers, resting your palms on the top of your head.

3 Exhale, slowly pulling your chin down toward your chest and aiming to keep your upper back in contact with the floor.

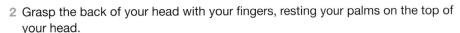

? REVIEW QUESTIONS

1 What is meant by an active, healthy and balanced lifestyle; for example, for a teenager.

2 How might this change for someone who is over 60 years of age?

3 What are the health-related components of fitness? Give practical examples for each.

4 For each health-related component explain how following an active, healthy lifestyle can make it more effective.

EXAM-STYLE QUESTIONS

Multiple choice questions

1 Cardiovascular endurance is a component of fitness and a healthy balanced lifestyle. Which of the following describes most accurately cardiovascular endurance:
   a the ability of our heart and lungs to cope with exercise over a long period of time
   b the ability to use muscles over a long period of time without them getting tired
   c the amount of force a muscle can exert against a resistance over a long period of time
   d the ability to change the body's movement quickly over a long period of time.

2 Hypertrophy is an increase in:
   a muscle size due to increased physical activity
   b lung capacity due to increased physical activity
   c cardiac output due to increased physical activity
   d calcium production due to increased physical activity.

Short answer questions

1 Identify three reasons why it is good to follow an active, healthy lifestyle. **(3 marks)**
2 Explain how our flexibility might be affected by our lifestyle choices. **(4 marks)**

WHAT YOU NEED TO KNOW

- the names of the health-related fitness components
- examples of how these might be used in everyday life and in a physical activity (SC)
- how a healthy, active and balanced lifestyle can enhance these components and make them more efficient and effective (SC)
- importance of the warm-up and cool-down with practical examples. (SC)

4.2 HOW PHYSICAL ACTIVITY IMPACTS ON THE DEVELOPMENT OF THE SKELETAL SYSTEM

LEARNING GOALS

By the end of this section you should be able to:

- identify and describe the main functions of the skeleton
- explain how physical activity and healthy lifestyles affect the skeleton and related joints
- identify and describe the structure of different types of joint
- describe the hinge joint and the ball and socket joint, and give examples of the articulating bones associated with these joints
- identify the different ranges of movement that are allowed by joints
- describe the problems that can be experienced with joints and how to avoid them.

THE FUNCTIONS OF THE SKELETON AS PART OF A HEALTHY, ACTIVE BODY

The skeleton has five major functions:

1 to give shape and support to the body, therefore enabling good posture
2 to allow movement of the body by providing sites for muscle attachment and a system of levers
3 to protect the internal organs such as heart, lungs, spinal cord and brain
4 to produce red and white blood cells
5 to store minerals.

PRACTICAL APPLICATIONS

For us to be able to carry out everyday activities such as picking things up and moving around, as well as participating in physical activities, we need to be able to use the levers that our skeletal system provides.

The axial skeleton is the main source of support and is the central part of the skeleton. It includes the cranium, the vertebral column and the rib cage comprising twelve pairs of ribs and the sternum.

The appendicular skeleton consists of the remaining bones and includes the girdles that join these bones on to the axial skeleton.

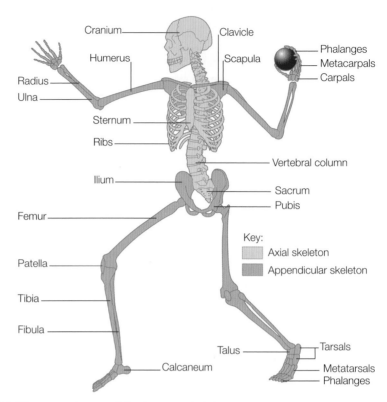

Fig 4.2.1 The major bones of the human skeleton

 **ACTIVITY 2**

TASK
Write the names of the major bones of the body on separate post-its. With a partner put each post-it on the appropriate area of the body.

CHALLENGE
Do the same as above but with the major joints of the body.

TYPES OF JOINT

There are many different types of joint in the human body, including some that allow little or no movement. The three main types of joint are:

Fibrous or fixed

These do not allow any movement. There is tough, fibrous tissue between the ends of the bones, e.g. the sutures of the cranium.

Cartilaginous or slightly moveable

These allow some movement. The ends of the bones have tough, fibrous cartilage, which allows for shock absorption but also gives stability, e.g. the intervertebral discs in the spine.

Synovial or freely moveable

This is the most common joint and since it allows for a wide range of movement is very important to sports participants. It consists of a joint capsule lined with a synovial membrane. Lubrication is provided for the joint in the form of synovial fluid secreted by the synovial membrane, e.g. knee joint.

Synovial joints can be subdivided into several further categories.

Hinge joint
This allows movement in one plane only (uniaxial), e.g. knee joint.

 PRACTICAL APPLICATION

An example of a physical activity that uses a hinge joint is sprinting.

Fig 4.2.2 The knee joint is used extensively in sport and exercise

Pivot joint
This allows rotation only and is therefore also uniaxial, e.g. axis and atlas bones of the cervical vertebrae.

 PRACTICAL APPLICATION

An example of a physical activity that uses a pivot joint is turning the head to find a fellow player to pass to in hockey.

Ellipsoid
e.g., radio-carpal joint

Fig 4.2.3

Ellipsoid joint
This is biaxial, allowing movement in two planes, e.g. the radio-carpal joint of the wrist.

 PRACTICAL APPLICATION

An example of a physical activity that uses an ellipsoid joint is playing a forehand clear in badminton.

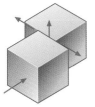

Gliding joint
e.g., carpals

Fig 4.2.4

Gliding joint
This is when two flat surfaces glide over one another and can permit movement in most directions, although mainly biaxial, e.g. the carpel bones in the wrist.

 PRACTICAL APPLICATION

An example of a physical activity that uses a gliding joint is dribbling the ball by moving the hockey stick over and back.

Saddle joint
e.g., carpo-meta carpal joint of thumb

Fig 4.2.5

Saddle joint
This is when a concave surface meets a convex surface and is biaxial, e.g. carpal-metacarpal joint of the thumb.

 PRACTICAL APPLICATION

An example of a physical activity that uses a saddle joint is gripping a tennis racket with the thumb.

Ball and socket joint
e.g., hip joint

Fig 4.2.6

Ball and socket joint

This allows a wide range of movement and occurs when a round head of bone fits into a cup-shaped depression, e.g. the shoulder joint.

PRACTICAL APPLICATION

An example of a physical activity that uses a ball and socket joint is an athlete throwing a javelin.

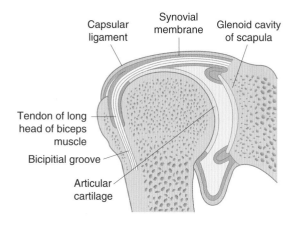

Capsular ligament — Synovial membrane — Glenoid cavity of scapula

Tendon of long head of biceps muscle

Bicipitial groove

Articular cartilage

Fig 4.2.7 A thrower needs a healthy and strong shoulder joint

Make sure that you can describe the hinge joint and the ball and socket joint in particular because these are singled out in the specification. You need to be able to identify an example of each and describe a movement that is associated with the use of each of these two joints.

Cartilage

This is soft connective tissue. Newly born babies have a skeleton consisting of cartilage and as they get older this cartilage is mostly replaced by bone – a process known as 'ossification'. Cartilage has no blood supply but receives nutrition though diffusion from the surrounding capillary network. There are three basic types of cartilage.

Yellow elastic cartilage
This is flexible tissue, e.g. part of the ear lobe.

Hyaline or blue articular cartilage
This is found on the articulating surfaces of bones. It performs a protective function by allowing movement between bones with limited friction. Hyaline cartilage thickens as a result of exercise.

White fibro-cartilage
This consists of tough tissue that acts as a shock absorber. It is found in parts of the body where there is a great amount of stress, for example the semi-lunar cartilage in the knee joint.

PRACTICAL APPLICATION

You can tear a cartilage by a forceful knee movement whilst you are weight-bearing on the same leg. For example a footballer may twist the knee whilst the foot is still on the ground – for instance, whilst dribbling round a defender. Another example is a tennis player who twists to hit a ball hard, while keeping their foot in the same position.

Sometimes a tear develops due to repeated small injuries to the cartilage, or owing to degeneration ('wear and tear') of the meniscus cartilage in older people. In severe injuries, other parts of the knee may also be damaged in addition to a meniscus tear. For example, you may also sprain or tear a ligament.

The cartilage does not heal very well once it is torn. This is mainly because it does not have a good blood supply. Small outer tears may heal in time, but larger tears, or a tear in the middle of the knee cartilage, tend not to heal properly.

Ligaments

These are bands of connective tissue between bones. They are very tough and resilient and help to join bones together and keep them stable. Some ligaments form the synovial capsule, while others are outside the capsule. The ligaments prevent extreme movements and help stop dislocation.

Levers

Levers add efficiency and force to the body's movements. They are made up of a lever arm, a fulcrum that is the pivot point, a load force and an effort force. There are three types of levers.

First-class levers
The fulcrum is located between the effort force and the load force on the lever arm. An example of this type of lever is the neck joint.

Second-class levers
This is when the resistance is between the fulcrum and the effort. If you rise up on your toes or plantar flex your ankles, this lever is in operation.

Third-class levers
This is when the effort is between the fulcrum and the resistance. This is the most common form of lever in the human body.

RANGES OF MOVEMENT

Flexion

This refers to a decrease in the angle around a joint, e.g. bend your arm at the elbow and touch your shoulder with your hand.

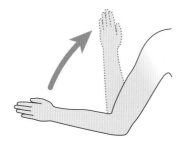

PRACTICAL APPLICATION

When a badminton player hits a forehand the arm shows flexion at the elbow.

Extension

This is when the angle of the bones that are moving (articulating bones) is increased, e.g. when standing up from a stooped or squat position. The angle between your femur and tibia (upper and lower leg) increases, thus extension has taken place.

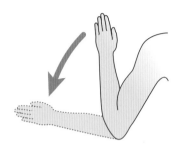

Fig 4.2.8 A basketball player extending his legs as he drives up to the basket

 PRACTICAL APPLICATION

When a basketball player drives up to the basket from bent legs to straight, **extension** occurs at the knee joint.

Abduction

The movement of the body away from the middle or the midline of the body, e.g. lying on your left side and lifting your right leg straight up, away from the midline.

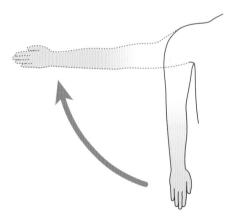

PRACTICAL APPLICATION

A gymnast with their leg lifted to the side of their body shows **abduction**.

Fig 4.2.9 A gymnast with her leg held to the side of her body, showing extension

Adduction

This is the opposite of abduction and is the movement towards the midline, e.g. lowering your lifted leg towards the middle of your body.

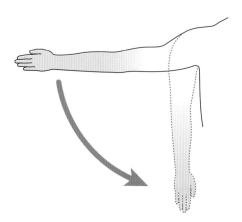

 PRACTICAL APPLICATION

In swimming the recovery of the legs from the breaststroke leg kick involves **adduction**.

Fig 4.2.10 A swimmer showing a leg kick while doing the breaststroke

Rotation

This is when the bone turns about its longitudinal axis within the joint. Rotation towards the body is called internal or **medial rotation**; rotation away from the body is called external or **lateral rotation.**

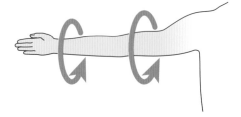

Fig 4.2.11 A ballet dancer rotating her hip joint laterally while dancing

PRACTICAL APPLICATIONS

A ballet dancer moving into first position **rotates** the hip joint laterally.

The articulating bones associated with the hinge joint and the ball and socket joint.

An example of a hinge joint is the knee joint.

The movements allowed by this joint are flexion and extension.

The articulating bones for the knee joint are the femur and the tibia.

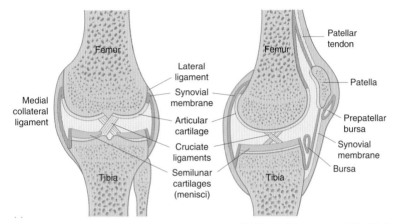

Fig 4.2.12 Knee joint viewed from the rear (left) and from the side (right)

An example of a ball and socket joint is the hip joint.

The movements allowed by the hip joint are flexion, extension, abduction, adduction, rotation and circumduction (this last movement is not in the specification).

The articulating bones for the hip joint are the femur and the pelvis.

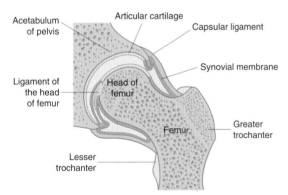

Fig 4.2.13 The hip joint viewed from the front

ACTIVITY 3

TASK

Draw the knee joint and the hip joint and label the bones that move around each joint.

Name a physical activity that involves both flexion and extension of the knee joint.

CHALLENGE

Draw the hip joint and label the bones that move around this joint.

Describe a skill in a physical activity that involves both abduction and adduction of the joint.

www.kidsexercise.co.uk
Includes useful
information about
reducing joint
problems with
exercise.

www.arthritiscare.org.uk
More information
about arthritis and its
treatment.

PROBLEMS ASSOCIATED WITH JOINTS

Various problems are associated with joints, and some of them can be avoided through an active, healthy lifestyle.

The skeletal system's response to exercise

Exercise has short- and long-term effects on the skeleton.

In terms of short-term changes in joints, movement stimulates the secretion of synovial fluid. The synovial fluid becomes less viscous, which enables a greater range of movement, in other words the joint appears to get 'looser'.

In the longer term and with more persistent exercise, the connective tissue around the skeleton becomes more flexible. Over a period of time the short-term improvement in the range of movement becomes more sustained.

Skeletal bone increases in its density as a result of exercise. This makes the bones stronger and can help to offset the effects of bone disease such as osteoporosis.

Hyaline cartilage also thickens with exercise, which helps to cushion the joint, therefore preventing damage to the bone. Tendons thicken and the ligaments have a greater stretch potential, again helping to protect the body from injury.

The bone mineral content of calcium and phosphate has been shown to be significantly higher in those who participate in regular exercise for all ages than those who do not. This is a compelling reason for regular exercise for all, including the elderly.

Arthritis

Arthritis means inflammation of the joints. Over 9 million people in the UK have arthritis and most of them will experience pain and difficulty moving around. However, people with arthritis can take control of their symptoms and continue to have a good quality of life.

Two of the most common forms of arthritis are osteoarthritis and rheumatoid arthritis.

Osteoarthritis is usually a result of aging and general wear and tear, but can be a consequence of injury during exercise or of being overweight.

Rheumatoid arthritis (RA) is when a person's immune system attacks cells within the joint capsule. It can destroy cartilage, ligaments and bone. If you are female you are more likely to get RA. There are genetic links that may predispose you towards the disease. If you smoke or are obese this also increases your chances of getting RA.

Arthritis is not just a disease of older people – it can affect people of all ages, including children. It is not clear what causes arthritis and unfortunately there is no cure at present. However, an active, healthy lifestyle can help those suffering from this disease.

General reduction of stress on joints can be achieved by:

- keeping to your ideal weight – eat a balanced, healthy diet
- spacing out your physical tasks so that you perform them at intervals, not all at the same time
- wearing shoes that have plenty of cushioning, especially when exercising.

Osteoporosis

Osteoporosis
Osteoporosis is a disease in which bones become fragile and more likely to break.

Osteoporosis occurs when the body fails to form enough new bone, or too much old bone is reabsorbed, or both. Two essential minerals for normal bone formation are calcium and phosphate.

The leading cause of osteoporosis is a lack of certain hormones, particularly oestrogen in women. Women aged over 60 years are frequently diagnosed with the disease. Other factors that may contribute to bone loss in this age group include inadequate intake of calcium and vitamin D and a lack of weight-bearing exercise.

If not prevented or if left untreated, osteoporosis can progress painlessly until a bone breaks. These broken bones, also known as fractures, occur typically in the hip, spine and wrist.

Fig 4.2.14 Exercise can combat bone disease such as osteoporosis

? REVIEW QUESTIONS

1 What are the main functions of the skeleton?
2 Where is a hinge joint found?
3 Where is a ball and socket joint found?
4 What does cartilage do?
5 What are the main effects of osteoporosis?
6 How can regular exercise help combat this disease?
7 What sort of activities would you advise elderly people to undertake in order to experience positive effects of exercise on the skeletal system?

EXAM-STYLE QUESTIONS

Multiple choice questions

1 One of the functions of the human skeleton as part of a healthy, active body is to provide:
   a oxygen to the body
   b protection to the internal organs
   c a source of vitamins
   d warmth for the body.

2 A good example of a hinge joint would be:
   a knee
   b shoulder
   c hip
   d ankle.

Short answer questions

1 Why is it important to have healthy joints?   **(2 marks)**
2 What aspects of lifestyle could affect the health of bones and joints?   **(4 marks)**
3 Name a specific joint problem and describe how you would try to
   avoid such problems.   **(4 marks)**

 WHAT YOU NEED TO KNOW

- the main functions of the skeleton including lever action
- how physical activity impacts on the development of the skeletal system
- the structure of the hinge joint and ball and socket joint, with examples
- the operation of the hinge joint and ball and socket joint in terms of flexion, extension, rotation, abduction and adduction, with examples
- the articulating bones associated with a hinge joint and a ball and socket joint
- the structure and function of ligaments and cartilage with associated problems and how to avoid them
- problems with joints and how to try to avoid them.

4.3 THE WAYS IN WHICH AN ACTIVE, HEALTHY LIFESTYLE CAN AFFECT MUSCLES

 LEARNING GOALS

By the end of this section you should be able to:

- identify and describe the composition of skeletal muscle
- identify the major muscle groups and explain how a healthy lifestyle can maintain and develop muscles
- describe the roles of muscles in movement
- describe aerobic and anaerobic exercise and how they can develop participation and performance
- describe the role and function of tendons
- explain how an active healthy lifestyle can help to avoid problems with muscles and tendons.
- explain the effects of lactic acid.

The specification states that candidates should be able to:
- identify of ways in which an active, healthy lifestyle can maintain and develop the health of muscles
- apply these via practical examples
- show understanding of which of the major muscle groups (deltoid; trapezius; latissimus dorsi; pectorals; biceps; triceps; abdominals; quadriceps; hamstrings) are involved in and benefit from particular types of physical activity.

MUSCULAR SYSTEM

Types of muscle

Involuntary muscle

Also known as smooth muscle, this is found in the body's internal organs. It is involuntary muscle, i.e. it is not under our conscious control.

Cardiac muscle

This is only found in the heart and is also involuntary.

Skeletal or voluntary muscle

This is under our conscious control and is used primarily for movement.

The functions of specific muscles

The following muscle are named in the specification:

Triceps

This is the elbow extensor (*triceps brachii*) and is attached to the elbow. Its function is to straighten the elbow and swing the arm backwards, e.g. backhand in table tennis.

Biceps

This is an elbow flexor (*biceps brachii*). Its function is to swing the upper arm forward and turn the forearm so that the palm of the hand points upwards (supination), e.g biceps curl in weight training.

Deltoid

This is used in all movements of the arms. Its most important function is to lift the arm straight outwards and upwards (abduction), e.g. to make a block in volleyball with arms straight above the head.

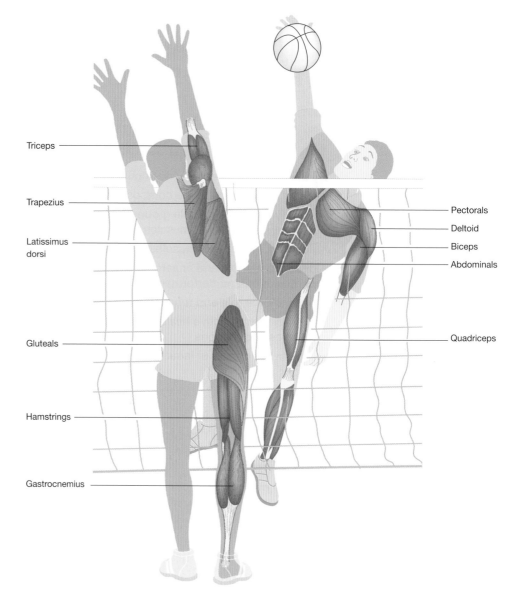

Triceps

Trapezius

Latissimus
dorsi

Gluteals

Hamstrings

Gastrocnemius

Pectorals

Deltoid

Biceps

Abdominals

Quadriceps

Fig 4.3.1 The Muscular System

Pectorals

There are two sets of chest muscles: *pectoralis major* (greater chest muscle) and *pectoralis minor* (lesser chest muscle). These help to adduct the arm and rotate it inwards as well as lowering the shoulder blades; for example, a rugby player making a tackle would hold on to their opponent using the pectoral muscles.

Trapezius

This adducts and rotates the shoulder blade outwards. It also helps to turn the head and bends the neck backwards; for example, a rugby forward in a scrum will use the trapezius to bind into the opponents (in other words, to establish a hold on to an opponent's upper body in a scrum).

Gluteals
These are the muscles in your buttocks. They straighten and adduct the hip, rotate the thigh outwards and help to straighten the knee. For example, a sprinter will use the gluteals in the leg action of sprinting down the track.

Quadriceps
This provides stability to the knee joint and extends or straightens the knee joint; for example, a long jumper when driving off the board will straighten the knee joint at take-off using the quadriceps.

Hamstrings
These muscles will straighten the hip. They will also bend the knee and rotate it outwards; for example, a hockey player when running across the pitch will be using her hamstrings in the running action to bend the knees.

Gastrocnemius
Usually known as the calf muscle, this is used to bend the knee and straighten or plantar-flex the ankle; for example, a swimmer doing front crawl will point their toes in the leg action using the *gastrocnemius*.

Fig 4.3.2 A hockey player when running across the pitch will be using her hamstrings in the running action to bend her knees.

Latissimus dorsi
The broad back muscle, which will swing the arm backwards and rotate it inwards; for example, a tennis player when serving swings their arm back to hit the ball and is using the *latissimus dorsi*.

Abdominals
These bend the trunk forwards and help to turn the upper body; for example, performing a sit-up exercise will use the abdominals.

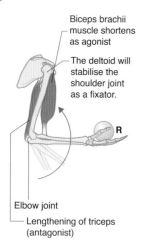

Biceps brachii muscle shortens as agonist

The deltoid will stabilise the shoulder joint as a fixator.

R

Elbow joint

Lengthening of triceps (antagonist)

Fig 4.3.3 Flexion at elbow with agonist labelled

Fixator
This is a muscle that works with others to stabilise the origin of the prime mover; for example, the trapezius contracts to stabilise the origin of the biceps.

Origin
This is the end of the muscle attached to a bone that is stable, e.g. the scapula. The point of origin remains still when contraction occurs. Some muscles have two or more origins; for example, the biceps muscle has two heads that pull on one insertion to lift the lower arm.

Insertion
This is the end of the muscle attached to the bone that actively moves; for example, the biceps insertion is on the radius.

Pairs of muscles

A vast range of movements can be made by the human body To produce these movements, muscles either shorten, lengthen or remain the same length when they contract. Muscles work in pairs. As one muscle contracts the other relaxes. Muscles that work together like this are called **antagonistic pairs.** This type of action enables the body to move with stability and control.

Examples of antagonistic pairs are:
- Biceps and triceps – at the arm joint. As the biceps bend the arms by contracting, the triceps relax. As the arm straightens the opposite occurs.
- Hamstrings and quadriceps – at the knee joint. The hamstrings contract and the quadriceps relax and the knee bends. As the knee straightens the quads contract and the hamstrings relax.

Agonist
This is the muscle that produces the desired joint movement and is also known as the **prime mover.** For example, the biceps brachii is the muscle that produces flexion movement at the elbow.

Antagonist
For movement to be co-ordinated muscles work in pairs so that control is maintained. The movement caused by the agonist is countered by the action of the opposing muscle called the antagonist; for example, the action at the elbow caused by the biceps shortening is opposed by the lengthening of the triceps, which acts as the antagonist.

ROLE AND FUNCTION OF TENDONS

Muscles are attached to bones via tendons. These are strong and can be slightly flexible. They help to apply the power needed to move bones.

If contraction is excessively strong then tendons can be damaged; for example, to the Achilles tendon in the lower leg. If the tendon is damaged below the knee, often caused by over-training, it could cause the onset of Osgood-Schlatter's disease.

An active, healthy lifestyle entailing a balanced amount and type of exercise can limit tendon damage. Exercise can strengthen tendons and make them more flexible and less prone to injury.

Tendonitis
Tendonitis means inflammation of a tendon. Symptoms are:
- tenderness
- pain
- swelling
- skin may be warm
- reduced movement of the muscle(s) that are pulled by the inflamed tendon.

In some cases the inflammation lasts just a few days and then goes away on its own. In others it can last weeks or months if not treated.

PRACTICAL APPLICATIONS
Certain types of exercise can render some areas of the body more prone to tendonitis. Tendons over the wrist and hand are the most commonly affected.

Synergists
These are muscles that actively help the prime mover or agonist to produce the desired movement. They are sometimes called **neutralisers** because they prevent any undesired movements. For example, the *brachialis* acts as a synergist when the elbow is bent and the forearm moves upwards. Sometimes the fixator and the synergist are the same muscle.

The specification states that problems associated with tendons need to be described, along with details of how to avoid them.

How to avoid problems with tendons:

- Avoid repetitive movements and overuse of the affected area.
- Exercises to strengthen the muscles around the affected tendon may help (seek advice from a physiotherapist).
- Seek appropriate treatment (medical advice may be necessary).
- Rest the affected part.

It is important to allow the inflammation to settle. Sometimes a bandage is put on a wrist if this is the area affected. This enables the hands and wrist to stay in the same position, thus allowing rest of the affected tendon.

The use of ice packs over the affected area may ease swelling and pain.

Anti-inflammatory painkillers are often prescribed (for example, ibuprofen). These ease pain and reduce inflammation.

Physiotherapy may be advised, especially if the condition is not settling with the above measures.

A steroid injection into the site of inflammation may be given if the above measures do not work. Steroids work by reducing inflammation and are usually effective.

Surgical release of a tendon is needed in very extreme cases.

Antibiotics are needed in the uncommon situation where infection is the cause of tendonitis.

Tennis elbow

This is a very painful injury that occurs to the outside of the elbow where the tendons that cock the wrist become inflamed. These tendons attach to the bony part of the outer elbow bone called the *lateral epicondyle*. The scientific name for the injury is *lateral epicondylitis*, meaning inflammation to the outside elbow bone. We refer to it as tennis elbow as tennis players are the main sufferers.

Fig 4.3.4 The scientific name for tennis elbow is *lateral epicondylitis*, meaning inflammation to the outside of the elbow bone. It gets its common name from the fact that it is mainly suffered by tennis players.

Tennis elbow is caused by the repetitive movement of hitting thousands and thousands of tennis balls. The main cause of the injury is playing too much, but other reasons may be equipment-related, such as too large a handle or a racket that is strung too tightly.

Tiny tears develop in the forearm tendon attachment at the elbow. The pain starts slowly but increases to a point where hitting the ball, especially a backhand shot, becomes virtually impossible. If you rest your arm when the discomfort first appears, the micro tears will heal. However, if you keep on playing, the micro tears will become bigger, eventually causing pain and swelling that prevents you from hitting a ball altogether. Pain can stretch down your forearm to your hand and simple actions like holding a cup of tea or carrying a bag become painful, forcing you to use your other hand.

To treat this condition, the first thing to do is rest from tennis completely to allow the micro tears to heal. Other measures involve a combination of:

- ice to reduce swelling
- anti-inflammatory tablets from your doctor
- soft tissue massage to the tight forearm muscles and the injured tendons once the pain has gone down
- stretching the forearm muscles to help blood flow
- tissue-healing ultrasound therapy
- strengthening exercises for the forearm muscles and tendons.

Sometimes top tennis stars require cortisone injections or an operation if the injury doesn't respond to rest and physiotherapy.

Strengthening your forearm muscles, which grip the racket and stiffen the wrist during backhand shots, should help to prevent the injury from happening again. Stretch the forearm muscles and tendons when warming up. You may want to try an elbow brace to take the pressure off the injured tendon.

Technique adjustments may also help; for example, try playing the backhand shot more from the shoulders and less from the wrist. Also, try to reduce the number of straight-arm shots you play by bending your arm at the elbow. This will bring the shoulder and arm muscles more into play and take the pressure off the wrist.

THE EFFECTS OF LACTIC ACID

The specification states that you need to know how lactic acid can affect exercise, training and the ability to keep going.

After a prolonged period of exercise (which uses up oxygen) there is an absence of oxygen in the muscles and lactic acid is formed in the working muscles. Lactic acid causes muscle pain and often this leads us to stop or reduce the activity we are doing. In other words, the uncomfortable build-up of lactic acid means we cannot continue exercising for long. When we recover, we take in oxygen and this helps to convert lactic acid into waste products that we can get rid of.

An active, healthy lifestyle will:

- improve the muscles' capability of using oxygen more efficiently
- help muscles deal with larger amounts of lactic acid
- ensure that we can keep going for longer in activities and physical work

Smoking and alcohol consumption will slow down our ability to deal with lactic acid.

MENTAL PREPARATION

Mental preparation is in the long course and you may be asked to explain how mental preparation can control emotions and improve people's ability to play and exercise fairly and cope with stress.

Mental – preparation techniques are widely used by those who participate in physical activities (as well as sportsmen and women) to cope with high levels of anxiety.

Cognitive anxiety-management techniques are those that affect the mind and therefore psychological anxiety. Somatic techniques (such as relaxation) are those that affect the body directly. Cognitive can affect somatic, and vice versa.

PRACTICAL APPLICATIONS

Controlling the heart rate by relaxation methods can make us feel more positive about performing. Positive thinking can, in turn, control our heart rate.

The following stress-management techniques can be used as coping strategies.

Imagery

Imagery involves the creation of pictures in our minds. Many people try to get the feeling of movement or capture an emotion through imagery. Imagery can improve concentration and confidence.

PRACTICAL APPLICATIONS

A winter Olympic athlete who is responsible for steering the team's bobsleigh visualises or uses imagery to picture the track, with all its bends, twists and turns. He goes through the movements he has to perform when he pictures each aspect of the run in his mind. This is an example of imagery or 'mental rehearsal'.

Imagery can also help with relaxation. When participants in a physical activity or performers in sport feel anxious, they sometimes go to 'another place' in their minds to try and calm down. Many people report that they use this technique to cope with stress and anxiety.

External imagery

This is when you can picture yourself from outside your body, like watching yourself on film; for example, a racing-car driver may go through the route in their mind before the race.

Internal imagery

This is when you imagine yourself doing the activity and can simulate the feeling of it, as in the bobsleigh example above or when a high jumper visualises the whole activity of run-up, jump and landing.

Fig 4.3.5 Visualising before a jump

PRACTICAL APPLICATIONS

To be effective in using imagery you need to take the following points into consideration:

- Relax in a comfortable, warm setting before you attempt to practise imagery.
- If you want to improve a skill by using imagery, then practise in a real-life situation.
- Imagery exercises should be short but frequent.
- Set goals for each session, e.g. concentrate on imagining the feel of a tennis serve in one short session.
- Construct a programme for your training in imagery.
- Evaluate your programme at regular intervals. Use the sports imagery evaluation to help to assess your training.

www.mindtools.com
Provides strategies for self-motivation and anxiety control.

www.athleticinsight.com
Provides information about mental preparation for athletes.

Self-talk

This technique involves participants and performers being positive about past experiences and performances and future efforts by talking to themselves. This technique has been shown to help with self-confidence and to raise levels of aspiration. Unfortunately self-talk is often used negatively. It is very common for sports performers to 'talk themselves out of winning' – for instance, a penalty taker saying to herself 'I will probably miss this'. It is also very common for young people to say that they don't want to exercise because they might look foolish or be embarrassed in front of others. This is known as negative self-talk and should be minimised in the interests of enthusiastic participation and good performance. High-level performers cannot afford to be negative and they must develop strategies to change these negative thoughts into positive ones.

There are thought to be five categories of negative thoughts:

1 Worry about performance, e.g. 'I am no good at this'.
2 Inability to make decisions, e.g. 'Shall I pass, shall I hold, shall I shoot?'
3 Preoccupation with physical feelings, e.g. 'I feel too tired, I'm going to give up and rest'.
4 Anxiety about what will happen if they lose, e.g. 'What will my coach say when I lose this point?'
5 Unfavourable comparisons with other people, e.g. 'He is better than me'.

 ACTIVITY 4

CHALLENGE
Construct a 6-week psychological skills training programme for a selected sports performer. Present your plan to the rest of the class.

RELAXATION

Somatic anxiety (the physical symptoms of anxiety, such as high heart rate) can lead to cognitive anxiety (mental anxiety, such as being worried), so the more physically relaxed you are, the better your chances of feeling mentally relaxed. There is, of course, a happy medium in physical activities: you don't want to be too laid back because you need to be dynamic and react quickly.

Relaxation exercises can be useful before you undertake training in mental exercises such as imagery. They help the sports person to be calmer and steadier before performance. Relaxation skills are like any other type of skill: you need to practise hard to achieve them.

Self-directed relaxation

Like other techniques this needs practice to be effective. Each muscle group is relaxed one at a time, and coaches can help teach the skills of self-directed relaxation; for example, through teaching breathing exercises. The athlete then practises without direct help. Eventually it will only take a very short time for full relaxation. This time factor is crucial if the athlete is to use the strategy just before or during competition.

Progressive relaxation training (PRT)

With this the athlete learns to be aware of the tension in the muscles and then releases all the tension. Because the athlete is so aware of the tension in the first place, they have a more effective sense of losing that tension when it goes.

PRT is sometimes referred to as the Jacobsen technique after the pioneer of the method.

Fig 4.3.6 An athlete relaxing muscles

 PRACTICAL APPLICATIONS

Using progressive relaxation training:
- Sit on the floor with your legs out straight in front of you.
- Now with your right leg, tense the muscles by pulling your toes up towards your knee using your leg and foot muscles.
- Develop as much tension as possible and hold for about 5 seconds and concentrate on what it feels like.
- Next completely relax your leg muscles and let your foot go floppy. Concentrate on what the relaxed muscles feel like.
- Now try to relax your muscles even more.
- By the end of the exercise your leg should feel far more relaxed than at the beginning.

 REVIEW QUESTIONS

1 Describe three types of muscle.
2 Where are the pectoral muscles and what do they do?
3 What are antagonistic pairs of muscles? Give an example of an antagonistic pair.
4 Give a simple description of aerobic exercise.
5 What are the effects of lactic acid?
6 Describe the role and functions of tendons.
7 What is meant by muscular hypertrophy?

EXAM-STYLE QUESTIONS

Multiple choice questions

1 A major muscle group that is responsible for movement around the shoulder is:
a biceps
b abdominals
c quadriceps
d deltoids.

2 Which of the following statements best describes the function of tendons?
a They attach muscle to muscle.
b They attach muscle to bone.
c They attach bone to bone.

3 A good example of a hinge joint would be:
a knee
b shoulder
c hip
d ankle.

4 The diagram shows a biceps curl with the lower arm moving towards the upper arm. Which of the following terms describes this movement?
a abduction
b adduction
c extension
d flexion

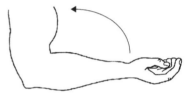

Short answer questions

1 Identify and describe three roles of the skeleton in physical activities.

(3 marks)

2 Give an example of a movement that shows flexion, and identify the major muscle groups involved.

(4 marks)

 WHAT YOU NEED TO KNOW

• the composition of skeletal muscle

• major muscle groups and examples of their actions

• how to keep muscles healthy

• the roles of muscles in movements

• the role and function of tendons

• the effects of lactic acid and how it affects the maintenance of physical activity

• the importance of mental preparation in controlling emotions, coping with stress and improving performance in physical activities.

CHAPTER 5

EVALUATING AND IMPROVING

LEARNING GOALS

By the end of this chapter you should be able to:

- describe the characteristics of skilful movement in physical activities sc
- identify and describe the differences between unskilled and skilled participants sc
- give practical examples of skilled movements in physical activities sc
- describe the nature of and differences between performance and outcome goals with practical examples for each sc
- explain the methods that help to assess the body's readiness for exercise and training sc
- identify and describe the structure and methods of tests for fitness and readiness for exercise. sc

THE CHARACTERISTICS OF SKILLED MOVEMENT

A skilled movement is one in which a predetermined objective is accomplished with maximum efficiency and a minimum outlay of energy.

When we talk of **skill**, we usually mean a combination of perceptual, cognitive and motor skills. But are skilful people born with their skills or do they learn them? The answer is probably a mixture of both. We all have abilities that are thought to be predetermined genetically; in other words, we are born with abilities and these influence our potential. But skills can also be acquired and improved; we should not expect sports-related skills to be ready-programmed in people's minds. The acquisition of fundamental motor skills is probably undervalued in a child's early development. If we can identify common actions that are needed for a range of different skills, we can teach them and enable learners to transfer them between skills and activities.

Skill

There are two main ways of using the word 'skill':

- to denote a specific task to be performed
- to describe the quality of a particular action, which might include how consistent the performance is and how well prepared the performer is to carry out the task.

ACTIVITY 1

TASK
Study a picture of a skilled performer in a physical activity. Write a list of words and phrases which you feel would describe such a performer.

Characteristics of skilful movement include the movement being *fluent*, *co-ordinated* and *controlled*. The performer *seems effortless* and *looks good* when they are performing the skill. There is obviously *good technique* being shown.

We often comment that an experienced sportsperson is 'skilful', but what do we actually mean by the word 'skill'? We use it to describe a task such as kicking a ball, but often we use it to describe the overall actions of someone who is good at what they do.

A movement skill is an action or task that has a goal and that requires voluntary body and/or limb movement to achieve the goal.

We know that top sportspeople are very fit but sometimes they don't seem to try very hard; their skill seems to come effortlessly and naturally. Whether it is a somersault in gymnastics or a perfectly timed rugby tackle, the skill looks good and is aesthetically pleasing. A skilled performer knows what he or she is trying to achieve and more often than not is successful, which is annoying if you are their opponent! A beginner, or novice, will seem clumsy and slow and will lack control. The novice will also tire quickly and expend more energy than is necessary.

PRACTICAL APPLICATIONS

If a tennis player often serves 'aces' in a match, we would label that player as skilled. If we watched him over a number of matches and he continued to serve aces, we would be more justified in labelling him as skilled. A squash player whom we might regard as skilled would anticipate where the ball is going to land and would put herself in a position to receive the ball early so that she could hit it early, thus placing her opponent at a disadvantage.

Sports players also have to assess the position of their teammates and opponents and decide where to pass the ball and how hard to pass it. This interpretation of information or stimuli is called **perception** and the skill required is called perceptual skill.

For skill acquisition to take place the person also needs **cognitive skills**. These skills are intellectually based and are linked to working out or solving problems; they underpin verbal reasoning. Such skills are often seen as innate, although there is considerable debate among psychologists as to how intelligence is acquired and whether there is only one or many ways in which people can show intelligence. For instance, is a football player showing intelligence when he selects a particular skill to be used in a particular situation?

ACTIVITY 2

TASK
Make a list of fundamental motor skills that you have learned.

CHALLENGE
Your physical activity, sport or exercise programme will require fundamental motor skills, more advanced motor skills and perceptual skills. Identify:
- the fundamental skills involved
- the motor skills involved
- any perceptual skills involved.

PERFORMANCE AND OUTCOME GOALS

Goal setting is widely used to motivate people to exercise and follow a healthy lifestyle. In sport, goal setting is a useful strategy for training and performance. Goal setting is a proven way of increasing motivation, increasing confidence and controlling anxiety.

There are two types of goal that can be recognised and set in sport.

For both the short and the long course you may be asked to describe performance and outcome goals and the differences between them and will need to be able to give practical examples for each.

Performance goals

These are directly related to the performance or technique of the activity. Performance goals in netball or football might be to improve passing or shooting techniques.

Fig 5.1 Performance goals in netball or football might be to improve passing or shooting techniques

Outcome goals

These are concerned with the end result – whether you win or lose, for instance. Outcome goals in netball or football might be to win an individual game or a tournament.

PRACTICAL APPLICATIONS

A golfer is trying to improve his driving swing and his timing; these are **performance goals**. A tennis player is trying to win the grand slam by winning each open tournament; these are **outcome goals**.

Outcome goals tend to be medium to long term, and performance goals tend to be short term.

Goals can affect performance in a number of ways, the main ones being:

1 They focus your attention and concentration.
2 They direct your efforts in a particular way.
3 They increase the amount of effort.
4 They are motivating to the performer, who often wants to develop a variety of strategies to be successful.

ACTIVITY 3

TASK

In one of your chosen physical activities, identify three performance goals and three outcome goals that you may have, or have had in the past.

CHALLENGE

Evaluate the goals you have identified above. Are these performance goals likely to be successful, or have they been successful and why? Are these outcome goals realistic and achievable? What other outcome goals might you identify if these three are achieved?

The specification includes the following specified tests and so the examiner can only ask direct questions about these. You are expected to be able to describe these assessments or tests and what they actually measure.
- health screening, including blood pressure and resting heart rate
- measurement of body mass index (BMI)
- suitable tests for cardiovascular endurance, e.g. the Cooper 12-minute run/walk test
- suitable tests for strength, e.g. the grip dynamometer test
- suitable tests for speed, e.g. the 30m sprint test
- suitable tests for flexibility, e.g. the sit and reach test

You are also expected to show an understanding of:
- the validity of tests and measurements
- how tests can take into account family history of relevant illnesses, and the participant's age, fitness levels, lifestyle and ability
- test protocols and Health and Safety considerations.

ASSESSING THE BODY'S READINESS FOR EXERCISE AND TRAINING

Assessing cardiovascular fitness

The level of endurance fitness is indicated by an individual's VO_2 max – that is the maximum amount of oxygen an individual can take in and utilise in one minute. The potential VO_2 max of an individual can be predicted via the **multistage fitness test** (sometimes called the 'bleep' or 'beep' test). This test involves a shuttle run that gets progressively more difficult.

The test is published by what was called the National Coaching Foundation (now Sports Coach UK) and is in the form of a CD. Subjects are required to run a 20m shuttle as many times as possible but ensuring that they turn at each end of the run in time with the 'bleep' on the tape. The time lapse between each bleep gets progressively shorter and so the shuttle run has to be completed progressively faster. At the point when the subject cannot keep up with the bleeps, they are deemed to have reached their optimum level. The test is now available from Sports Coach UK.

The level reached by the subject is recorded and used as a baseline for future tests or can be compared with national norms.

Safety factors:

- A person experiencing shortness of breath, chest pains, palpitations or light-headedness should stop exercising immediately and be sensitively advised to seek advice from a general practitioner.
- There is a need for the teacher or coach to exercise continuous observation of participants while the test is taking place, particularly of pupils known to be physically less fit.

(Source: Adapted from BAALPE Health and Safety guidelines)

National team scores on the multistage fitness test are shown in Table 5.1.

SPORT	MALE	FEMALE
Basketball	Level 11 – Shuttle 5	L9 – S6
Hockey	L13 – S9	L12 – S7
Rugby League	L13 – S1	
Netball		L9 – S7
Squash	L13 – S13	

Table 5.1

The multistage fitness test includes predictions of VO_2 max for individuals. Norms for VO_2 max for different age groups are shown in Tables 5.2 and 5.3.

	18–25 YEARS OLD	26–35 YEARS OLD	36–45 YEARS OLD	46–55 YEARS OLD	56–65 YEARS OLD	65+ YEARS OLD
Excellent	>60	>56	>51	>45	>41	>37
Good	52–60	49–56	43–51	39–45	36–41	33–37
Above average	47–51	43–48	39–42	35–38	32–35	29–32
Average	42–46	40–42	35–38	32–35	30–31	26–28
Below average	37–41	35–39	31–34	29–31	26–29	22–25
Poor	30–36	30–34	26–30	25–28	22–25	20–21
Very poor	<30	<30	<26	<25	<22	<20

Table 5.2 Maximal oxygen uptake norms for men (ml/kg/min)

	18–25 YEARS OLD	26–35 YEARS OLD	36–45 YEARS OLD	46–55 YEARS OLD	56–65 YEARS OLD	65+ YEARS OLD
Excellent	56	52	45	40	37	32
Good	47–56	45–52	38–45	34–40	32–37	28–32
Above average	42–46	39–44	34–37	31–33	28–31	25–27
Average	38–41	35–38	31–33	28–30	25–27	22–24
Below average	33–37	31–34	27–30	25–27	22–24	19–22
Poor	28–32	26–30	22–26	20–24	18–21	17–18
Very poor	<28	<26	<22	<20	<18	<17

Table 5.3 Maximal oxygen uptake norms for women (ml/kg/min)

PRACTICAL APPLICATIONS

David Beckham (football), Lance Armstrong (cycling) and Neil Back (England rugby player) are all rumoured to have achieved all 23 levels in the bleep test. Professional rugby flankers mostly score in the 12 to 13 range and prop forwards score around level 10. For females, the UK National Women's Rugby seven a side to Hong Kong in spring 2001 averaged over 11, with a range from 9 to 12.

An advantage of the multistage fitness test is that large groups of athletes can perform it together with few costs. Also, the test continues to maximum effort, unlike many other tests of endurance capacity which stop before maximum effort is reached.

The disadvantages are that: there are practice effects that can skew the results; the motivation levels of the subjects can influence the amount of effort expended; the scoring can be subjective, with some scorers being more lenient than others; and environmental conditions can affect the results, especially if the test is completed outside.

Assessing flexibility

Flexibility can be tested via the 'sit and reach test'. The objective of this test is to measure the athlete's lower back and hamstring flexibility. The subject sits on the floor with legs outstretched in a straight position. The subject reaches as far forward as possible but keeping the legs straight and in contact with the floor. The distance that the ends of the fingers are from the feet (pointing upwards) is measured. Using a 'sit and reach' box shown below ensures more accurate measurements. Once again this test provides measurements that can be used in assessing any future training and also for the subject to compare performance with national norms.

The national norms for 16 to 19 year olds are shown in Table 5.4.

GENDER	EXCELLENT	ABOVE AVERAGE	AVERAGE	BELOW AVERAGE	POOR
Male	>14 cm	11–14 cm	7–10 cm	4–6 cm	<4 cm
Female	>15 cm	12–15 cm	7–11 cm	4–6 cm	<4 cm

Table 5.4

The validity of the sit and reach test depends upon how strictly it is conducted and the individual's level of motivation. There are published tables to relate results to potential level of fitness and the correlation is high. This test only measures the flexibility of the lower back and hamstrings, and is a valid measure of this. The reliability depends on the amount of warm-up allowed, and whether the same procedures are followed each time.

The advantages of the sit and reach test are that there is extensive data to use for comparison, and it is a simple and quick test to administer and perform.

There are also some disadvantages, however. Variations in arm and leg length can obscure the results. Most norms are based on no previous warm-up, though the best results will be achieved after a warm-up or if the test is preceded by another test such as the endurance test. There is therefore a need for a consistent method of administrating the test.

PRACTICAL APPLICATIONS

Other fitness assessments include:

Assessing strength — use a grip dynaometer that assesses grip strength which is thought to be a good indication of overall upper body strength.
Assessing speed — the use of sprint tests over a measured distance, e.g. 30m.

Assessing body composition

Body composition can be assessed in a number of different ways.

Skinfold measurement

This is completed using a skinfold calliper (see Figure 5.2). Measurements are taken from the areas around the biceps, triceps, subscapular and supra iliac. The total measurements are added together and recorded to compare with national norms or more importantly to assess training or weight management programmes.

Measurement is usually from three to nine different anatomical sites around the body. The right side is usually the only side measured; this permits comparison with norms and helps individuals to ensure their own consistency in measurement. The tester pinches the skin at the appropriate site to raise a double layer of skin and the underlying adipose tissue, but does not include the muscle. The skinfold calipers are then used 1 cm below and at right angles to the pinch, and a reading is taken after two seconds. The mean of two separate measurements should be taken, again to ensure an accurate measurement.

Table 5.5 shows the percentage body fat for male and female athletes for named sports.

1. **Triceps brachii**
   With the pupil's arm hanging loosely, a vertical fold is raised at the back of the arm, midway along a line connecting the acromion (shoulder) and olecranon (elbow) processes.

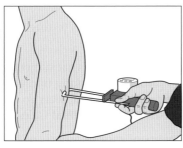

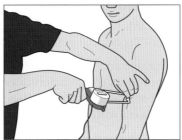

2. **Biceps brachii**
   A vertical fold is raised at the front of the arm, opposite to the triceps site. This should be directly above the centre of the cubital fossa (fold of the elbow).

3. **Subscapular**
   A fold is raised just beneath the inferior angle of the scapula (bottom of the shoulder-blade). This fold should be at an angle of 45 degrees downwards and outwards.

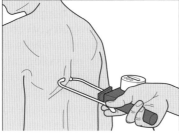

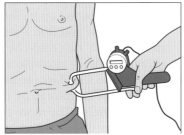

4. **Anterior suprailiac**
   A fold is raised 5–7 cm above the spinale (pelvis), at a point in line the anterior axillary border (armpit). The fold should be in line with the natural folds downward and inwards at up to 45 degrees.

Figure 5.2 Body fat measurements

SPORT	MALE	FEMALE
Baseball	12–15%	12–18%
Basketball	6–12%	20–27%
Canoe/kayak	6–12%	10–16%
Cycling	5–15%	15–20%
Field & ice hockey	8–15%	12–18%
Gymnastics	5–12%	10–16%
Rowing	6–14%	12–18%
Swimming	9–12%	14–24%
Tennis	12–16%	16–24%
Track – runners	8–10%	12–20%
Track – jumpers	7–12%	10–18%

Table 5.5

 PRACTICAL APPLICATIONS

It is recommended that men have 15-18% body fat and women have 20-25% body fat. Healthy male athletes might be as low as 5-12% body fat, and healthy female athletes could be as low as 10-20%.

Skinfold measurement is used extensively to assess body composition. It is simpler than other techniques such as hydrostatic weighing. Costs are minimal after the initial outlay for the skinfold callipers.

However, measurements often contain errors and therefore it is usually not appropriate to convert skinfold measures to percentage body fat. It is best to use the sum of several sites and to compare body fat measures from one period with another after a lapse of time.

The reliability of skinfold measurement can vary from tester to tester depending on their skill and experience.

www.screening.nhs.uk
An NHS website that gives more general information on health screening.

www.boxingscene.com
An interesting site on the need for screening for boxing.

Health screening

Health screening is an essential part of the fitness testing and training process for both sport and general exercise.

Fitness and exercise professionals always advise that subjects should get checked out by a general practitoner (GP) prior to embarking upon a new exercise regime. Health and leisure facilities should ensure that subjects go through the induction process with a qualified fitness instructor or personal trainer.

Conducting some initial assessments of various aspects of health and physical performance allows the subject and the professional to monitor progress. This screening process can include basic assessment of body composition, cholesterol, blood glucose and iron levels. If the subject's overall goal concerns weight management, this could be linked to a nutritional analysis. Health and fitness professionals are also able to monitor subjects' physiological responses to physical activity and therefore recommend specific effort levels based on heart rate, which can then be monitored by the subject or the health and fitness professional during exercise. The more elite the sportsmen/women, the more depth of analysis is necessary and this may include assessment of additional aspects specific to the sport, such as strength or power.

The following are typical health-screening measurements:

- body mass index (BMI)
- blood pressure
- cholesterol
- glucose
- resting heart rate
- hydration
- flexibility

Heart rate

When screening heart rate it is important to be familiar with the factors that affect it, including:

- stress
- illness
- time of day
- caffeine
- food
- alcohol
- altitude
- temperature
- cardiac drift

Cardiac drift
This is the increase in heart rate while you exercise with a constant workload. Your heart rate can increase by up to 20 beats per minute during exercise lasting from about 20 to 60 minutes even when workload/rate of work does not alter.

PRACTICAL APPLICATIONS

To calculate a client's resting heart rate (RHR):

- Find a quiet, private place for your assessment.
- Get the client to lie or sit down and to relax.

After 5–10 minutes take the pulse rate (beats/min) by using a heart rate monitor and use this as the client's resting heart rate.

Manual method

The manual or 'palpitation method' of measuring resting heart rate is used at the wrist (radial artery) and the neck (carotid artery).

To take your resting heart rate at the wrist, place your index and middle fingers together on the opposite wrist, about half an inch inside the joint, in line with the index finger. Feel for a pulse. When you find a pulse, count the number of beats you feel within a one-minute period. You can estimate the per-minute rate by counting over 10 seconds and multiplying this figure by 6, or over 15 seconds and multiplying by 4, or over 30 seconds and doubling the result.

You should always use your fingers to take a pulse, not your thumb, particularly when recording someone else's pulse, as you can sometimes feel your own pulse through your thumb.

Normal resting heart rates ranges anywhere from 40 beats per minute up to 100 beats per minute. Ideally you want to be between 60 and 90 beats per minute, with the average resting heart rate for a man being 70 beats per minute, and for a woman 75 beats per minute.

Blood pressure

A blood pressure measuring instrument called a sphygmomanometer is placed where the subject cannot see the results. Blood pressure is recorded first after the subject has rested quietly for 5 minutes. The client sits with an arm (recommended the left arm) resting, with the elbow approximately at the level of the heart. The cuff is attached, and the pressure is increased to approximately 180 mm Hg. The stethoscope is placed over the brachial artery in the cubital fossa. The pressure is released at a rate of approximately 2 mm per second. Both the pressure at which the first sound is heard (systolic pressure) and the pressure when all sounds disappear (diastolic pressure) are recorded.

Blood pressure is recorded in the units of millimetres of mercury (mm Hg). Normal blood pressure for men and women is usually considered to be 120 for systolic and 80 for diastolic pressure.

	ACCEPTABLE	BORDERLINE	HIGH
Systolic	< 140	140–160	> 160
Diastolic	< 85	85–95	> 95

Table 5.6 Normal blood pressure for men and women

It is common for blood pressure to increase in stressful conditions. If the subject seems stressed, it is important to repeat the test after they have relaxed. Medical referral should follow if measurements in the high category are recorded.

Body mass index

underweight	<20
healthy range	20–25
overweight	25–30
obese	>30

Table 5.7 BMI norms

The body mass index (BMI) is a measure of body composition. BMI is calculated by taking a person's weight and dividing it by their height squared.

The higher the BMI, the more body fat is present. However, this is only one indication and other issues such as body type should be taken into consideration.

The BMI does not apply to elderly people, pregnant women or highly trained athletes.

ACTIVITY 4

TASK
Assess your own fitness for exercise.
Which areas do you need to work on?

CHALLENGE
Obtain results of health screening questionnaires and health monitoring tests for two contrasting individuals:
1 a non-sports person aged 50
2 an active 16-year-old student.
Describe their fitness strengths and areas for fitness improvement.

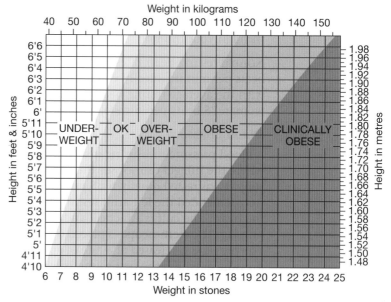

Fig 5.3 BMI chart

Source: www.best-weight-loss-and-fitness-programs.com

🎛 PRACTICAL APPLICATIONS

MULTISTAGE FITNESS TEST

Preparation

The written pre-test precautions provided with the test indicate the need for maximal effort if the test result is to be valid. Where there are doubts over the ability of any person to take part in the test, the coach should advise that medical advice is sought beforehand.

Individuals with an injury or illness should not undertake the test. Since the test starts very slowly, there is a gentle warm-up as the test progresses. However, in addition to this built-in warm-up feature, it is advisable for very light jogging and gentle stretching to be undertaken before commencing the shuttle runs.

Ideally, participants should be medically screened for the absence of cardiac abnormalities before they engage in vigorous sustained levels of physical activity.

For the test to be completed there must be a flat, non-slip surface, marking cones, a measuring tape, a pre-recorded CD with CD player recorder and recording sheets.

Purpose

The objective of the multistage fitness test (MSFT) is to monitor the development of the athlete's maximum oxygen uptake. The level of **endurance fitness** is indicated by an individual's **VO_2 max** – that is the maximum amount of oxygen an individual can take in and utilise in one minute. The potential VO_2 max of an individual can be predicted via this multistage fitness test.

CONDUCT OF THE TEST

- Measure and mark out a 20m area and mark each end with marker cones.
- The participant warms up by jogging and stretching.
- When the audiotape indicates, the participant starts to jog across the 20m area.
- The participant places one foot on or beyond the 20m markers at the end of each shuttle.
- If the participant arrives at the end of a shuttle before the bleep, the athlete must wait for the bleep and then start running again.
- The participant keeps running for as long as possible until he or she cannot keep up with the speed set by the tape, at which point they should stop.
- If the participant fails to reach the end of the shuttle before the bleep they should be allowed two or three further shuttles to attempt to regain the required pace before being stopped.
- Record the level and number of shuttles completed when the participant stops.
- At the end of the test, participants should warm down, including some stretching exercises.

Health and safety

Health and safety checks should be done before a testing session. These should include:

- checking for the proper working of equipment
- ensuring an adequate supply of safety equipment such as first aid kits
- giving adequate warm-up when necessary.

Maximal endurance testing of elderly and special populations should only be undertaken after medical clearance has been given. Medical assistance should be close at hand, and adequate resuscitation equipment should be available nearby.

Any person older than 35 years of age, particularly anyone overweight or with a history of high blood pressure and heart disease, should consult a medical practitioner before undertaking any vigorous testing.

All participants who are not accustomed to exercise should complete a Physical Readiness Questionnaire and be adequately health screened.

The testing process involves:

- identification of what is to be measured
- selection of a suitable method of measuring/test
- collection of data
- analysis of the data
- making decisions about an exercise or fitness programme
- implementation of the programme.

In selecting the test it is important to make sure that it is valid and appropriate to the person being tested. All tests should be:

- specific – designed to assess a participant's fitness for the activity/exercise purpose
- valid – it tests what it is supposed to test
- reliable – can the test be run in the same way again to achieve consistency?
- objective – produce a consistent result irrespective of the tester.

When you conduct tests the following points should be taken into consideration:

- Each test should measure one factor only.
- The test should not require any technical competence on the part of the participant – the simpler the better.
- The participant should understand what is required, what is being measured and why it is being measured.
- The test procedure should be strictly standardised to ensure consistency.

Results from testing a participant can be used to:

- create an appropriate training/exercise programme
- predict future performance/fitness levels
- indicate weaknesses
- measure improvement
- enable you to assess the success of training
- motivate the person

The following factors may impede the reliability of your tests:

- the amount of sleep the participant had prior to the test
- the participant's emotional state/level of motivation
- accuracy of measurements (times, distances, etc.)
- temperature, noise and humidity
- time of day and caffeine intake
- other people present – this can improve or impede results
- the skill of the tester.

REVIEW QUESTIONS

1 What is meant by skilful movement?
2 What are the differences between skilled and unskilled participants?
3 Why do we need to assess someone's readiness for exercise?
4 What is a common test for cardiovascular endurance?
5 What is a suitable flexibility test and how would you set it up?
6 What other factors would you take into consideration when assessing a person's readiness for exercise and training?
7 What health and safety implications are there when administering these assessments?

EXAM-STYLE QUESTIONS

Multiple choice questions

1 Skilled performers in physical education are different to unskilled performers because they:
   a try harder
   b are more outgoing
   c are more co-ordinated
   d try less hard.

2 Which of the following is a skill rather than an ability?
   a speed
   b catching
   c reaction time
   d balance.

3 Which one of the following shows incorrect information.
   a The multistage fitness test measures cardiovascular fitness.
   b Taking the pulse rate tests heart rate.
   c The sit and reach test measures flexibility.
   d The BMI tests speed.

4 The following are disadvantages of the sit and reach test except:
   a Variations in arm length can obscure the results
   b Variations in leg length can obscure the results
   c Some participants may warm up, some may not.
   d It is a simple test to administer.

Short answer questions

1 Using practical examples describe the differences between a skilled and unskilled participant.   **(4 marks)**

2 Describe a test for cardiovascular endurance and explain how you would implement it.   **(5 marks)**

3 What are the dangers of assessing someone's readiness for exercise?   **(4 marks)**

4 How would you test someone's flexibility?   **(2 marks)**

5 What is meant by the BMI and how does this give us information about a person's readiness for exercise?   **(5 marks)**

WHAT YOU NEED TO KNOW

- the characteristics of skilful movement in physical activities
- the differences between unskilled and skilled participants
- practical examples of skilled movements in physical activities
- the nature of and differences between performance and outcome goals with practical examples for each
- the structure of specific fitness tests
- the aspects of fitness that each test assesses
- the advantages and disadvantages of these assessments
- a range of other assessments related to body composition and readiness for exercise
- the health and safety implications of these assessments
- other aspects of health and lifestyle that should be taken into consideration when assessing readiness for exercise and training.

CHAPTER 6

HEALTHY, ACTIVE LIFESTYLES

6.1 MAKING INFORMED CHOICES ABOUT HEALTHY, ACTIVE LIFESTYLES

 LEARNING GOALS

By the end of this section you should be able to:

- describe the characteristics of a balanced, healthy lifestyle (SC)
- identify and describe the measures/indicators of health and well-being (SC)
- identify the components of a healthy diet and their functions (SC)
- explain the effects of age, gender and disability on participation and performance in physical activity (SC)
- describe the effects of smoking, alcohol, diet and performance-enhancing drugs on participation and performance in physical activity (SC)
- identify and describe methods of exercise for an active, healthy lifestyle (SC).

THE CHARACTERISTICS OF A BALANCED, HEALTHY LIFESTYLE

Many studies have revealed that a balanced, healthy lifestyle will help you to feel better and live longer. Taking exercise, not drinking too much alcohol, eating enough fruit and vegetables and not smoking can add up to 14 years to your life.

 PRACTICAL APPLICATIONS

Research involving 20,000 people over 10 years found those who did not follow a healthy lifestyle were four times more likely to have died than those who did. The findings held true regardless of how overweight or poor the people studied were.

The findings showed that it was in the reduction of deaths related to cardiovascular disease that people benefited most.

Source: *The Public Library of Science Medicine*, vol 3, No 10, 8 January, 2008.

A healthy, balanced lifestyle means different things to different people and in different cultures. Here in the UK there is general agreement that the following contribute to a healthy, balanced lifestyle:

- eating a healthy and balanced diet
- regular exercise – the current government recommendation is that adults should carry out a minimum of 30 minutes' moderate physical activity on five or more days a week, while children and young people aged 5–18 should participate in physical activity of moderate intensity for one hour a day
- maintaining a healthy body weight
- not smoking
- sensible alcohol consumption
- minimising stress.

An unhealthy lifestyle often includes the following:
- poor diet, e.g. excess fat, salt, sugar, protein and insufficient complex carbohydrate, vitamin/mineral and fluid intake
- inactivity and lack of exercise
- being overweight, which increases risk of certain types of cancers, high blood pressure, heart disease and diabetes
- smoking, which causes lung cancer, heart disease, chronic bronchitis, emphysema and is a risk factor for many cancers
- excess alcohol consumption, which increases risk of liver disease and mouth, throat and oesophageal (food pipe) cancer, and can contribute to obesity
- high stress levels, whether associated with work, ineffective time management, or general lifestyle habits.

The eatwell plate

FOOD
STANDARDS
AGENCY

food.gov.uk

Use the eatwell plate to help you get the balance right. It shows how much of what you eat should come from each food group.

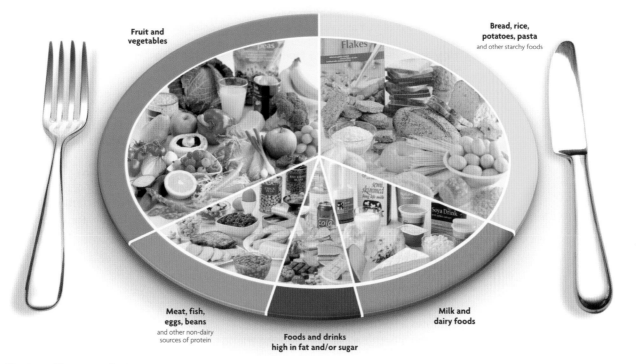

Fruit and vegetables

Bread, rice, potatoes, pasta
and other starchy foods

Meat, fish, eggs, beans
and other non-dairy sources of protein

Foods and drinks
high in fat and/or sugar

Milk and dairy foods

Fig 6.1.1 The eatwell plate
Source: Food Standards Agency

Below is a typical exam question and a hypothetical student response.

Question

1 Identify four reasons why it is good to follow an active, healthy lifestyle.

Student's answer

I would follow an active healthy lifestyle so that I don't suffer from illness and get colds all the time. I would also be able to play my sport of football well. It would also make me happy and I would enjoy life more.

Mark scheme

Four marks for four of the following:

1 to be able to exercise for long periods of time
2 any positive physiological adaptations (e.g. stronger heart/lungs)
3 to be able to recover quickly
4 to live longer/to be healthy/any identified health benefits/to avoid illness/heart attacks/problems/CHD
5 to make friends/socialise
6 to feel better/emotional benefits/enjoyment.

Commentary

The command word is 'identify', so candidates will be given credit by merely naming the reasons rather than having to give any description. This candidate has identified point 4 (less illness). Point 6 is achieved through the enjoyment aspect.

The candidate does not relate the point about playing sport well to the question. Total of 2 marks from the possible 4 marks.

 PRACTICAL APPLICATIONS

A healthy and balanced diet often means:
- five portions of fruit and vegetables each day
- high-fibre cereals and starchy foods
- small amounts of protein, fat, salt and sugar
- lots of water.

A healthy diet contributes to a healthy lifestyle by reducing the occurrence of certain cancers and the risk of high blood pressure. Heart disease is reduced, as is the risk of diabetes. A healthy diet can increase your energy levels and help you attain a healthy weight. There are psychological benefits too, linked with a favourable body image.

An active lifestyle often includes the following benefits:

- keeps the heart muscles in shape and makes the heart a more efficient pump
- increases blood flow and contributes to a reduction in risk factors for coronary heart disease
- reduces blood pressure
- reduces stress
- reduces diabetes risk
- increases 'good' cholesterol
- promotes a feeling of well-being
- promotes a better social life/making friends.

THE INDICATORS OF HEALTH AND WELL-BEING

> The examiner may ask for a description of these measures and indicators, along with practical examples; for example, being satisfied with life may include having a balance of healthy activities and a good worklife balance.

For us to be able to assess whether we are following a healthy, active, balanced lifestyle, we need to be able to measure the factors that make up such a lifestyle. The measurements (called 'indicators') give us a picture of how well we are doing, and an overall view of what we should be aiming for.

The indicators identified in the specification for GCSE PE are:

- **Satisfaction with aspects of life**. How satisfied do we feel about our lives overall? This does not mean that you will feel deliriously happy about everything but overall to be a healthy and balanced individual you need to be pretty satisfied with the way things are generally going.
- **Frequency of positive and negative feelings**. How often do you feel very positive about life around you and how often do you have negative thoughts? The more positive thoughts you have, the more healthy and balanced you are likely to be both mentally and physically.
- **Frequency of feelings or activities which may have a positive or negative impact on well-being.** Some of the feelings that you have or activities that you are involved in may have a real impact on how you feel; others often do not; for example, if you regularly play sport you may feel excited and enjoy being with others; this has a positive impact on the way you feel. If you are taking illegal drugs or are consuming too much alcohol this may also make you feel good in the short term but may have a lasting negative impact on your health and well-being.
- **Access to green space.** Do you have places around you that give you a sense of space? Those who live in overcrowded conditions and do not have anywhere around them that is spacious and has vegetation may well feel less good about their lives, which may have a negative impact on their health and well-being.
- **Level of participation in other activities.** Those who are active in many different ways are often the happiest. This is not always the case, but usually if you have a variety of interests then you have a better view of yourself and others.
- **Positive mental health.** If you feel happy, optimistic about the future and useful then you are more likely to have positive mental health. Those who are more relaxed, feel interested in other people and deal with problems well are also said to have positive mental health (see the activity below).

 ACTIVITY 1

TASK

Well-being: how do you feel?

Below are some statements about feelings and thoughts. Tick the statements that best describe your experience over the past two weeks.

- I've been feeling optimistic about the future.
- I've been feeling useful.
- I've been feeling relaxed.
- I've been feeling interested in other people.
- I've had energy to spare.
- I've been dealing with problems well.
- I've been thinking clearly.
- I've been feeling good about myself.

- I've been feeling close to other people.
- I've been feeling confident.
- I've been able to make up my own mind about things.
- I've been feeling loved.
- I've been interested in new things.
- I've been feeling cheerful.

Once you have thought about your responses, rate yourself out of 10 for how good you feel.

CHALLENGE

Are there any areas above that you have little control over, and if so what can you do?

THE HEALTHY DIET

> The examiner may ask for a description of a balanced, healthy diet, including hydration and getting a positive energy balance.

The following are the main nutrients or essential components the body requires to follow an active, healthy lifestyle.

Carbohydrates

These are made up of the chemical elements of carbon, hydrogen and oxygen. Carbohydrates are primarily involved in energy production. There are two forms of carbohydrate:

- simple sugars – these provide a quick energy source and include glucose and fructose
- complex starches – these have many sugar units and are much slower in releasing energy.

Carbohydrates are very important to the athlete, especially in exercise that is highly intense. They are also essential to the nervous system and determine fat metabolism.

Carbohydrates are stored in the muscles and the liver as glycogen but in limited amounts that need to be replenished.

PRACTICAL APPLICATIONS

Sources of carbohydrates include:
- complex – cereal, pasta, potatoes, bread, fruit.
- simple – sugar, jam, confectionery, fruit juices.

When exercise takes place, glycogen is broken down to glucose, which supplies muscles with energy. When glycogen stores are depleted, there is less energy available and the participant in exercise will become fatigued. The UK Department of Health Estimated Average Requirement (EAR) is a daily calorie intake of 1,940 calories per day for women and 2,550 for men. If you are eating 2,500 calories a day, the recommended daily intake of carbohydrate is at least 313 grams. For 2,000 calories it is at least 250g, and for 1,500 calories it is 188g.

It is recommended that about 60 per cent of an athlete's diet should consist of carbohydrates.

PRACTICAL APPLICATIONS

Leading up to the Beijing Olympics in 2008, the gold medallist swimmer Michael Phelps was reported to have eaten about 12,000 calories per day.

Saturated and unsaturated fats
A saturated fat is in the form of a solid, e.g. lard, and is primarily from animal sources. An unsaturated fat is in the form of liquid, e.g. vegetable oil, and comes from plant sources.

Obesity
The main measurement of obesity is the body mass index (BMI). This is your weight in kilograms divided by your height in metres squared. For example, someone who weighs 100 kilograms and is 1.8 metres tall has a BMI of 30.86 (100 divided by 3.25 [1.8 squared]). Individuals are defined as being overweight if their BMI is 25–30 and obese if their BMI is 30 or over.

  Obesity contributes to a range of problems, including heart disease, type 2 diabetes, osteoarthritis and some cancers. Experts say that obesity is as serious a health problem as smoking or excessive alcohol consumption.

Fats

These are also very important and are a major source of energy for athletes performing low-intensity endurance exercise. Fats or lipids are made up of carbon, hydrogen and oxygen but in different proportions to carbohydrates. There are two types:

- triglycerides – which are stored in the form of body fat
- fatty acids – which are used mainly as fuel for energy production; these are either saturated or unsaturated.

When muscles cells are readily supplied with oxygen, fat is the usual fuel for energy production. This is because the body is trying to save the limited stores of glycogen for high-intensity exercise and therefore delays the onset of fatigue. The body cannot solely use fat for energy and so the muscle is fuelled by a combination of fat and glycogen.

Fat consumption should be carefully monitored and can cause obesity. Fat is very important to protect vital organs and is crucial for cell production and the control of heat loss. It is generally accepted that a maximum of 3 per cent of total calories consumed should be from fatty foods.

Examples of sources of fats:

- saturated fats – meat products, dairy products, cakes, confectionery
- unsaturated fats – oily fish, nuts, margarine, olive oil.

Protein

Proteins are composed of carbon, hydrogen, oxygen and nitrogen and some contain minerals such as zinc. Proteins are known as the 'building blocks' for body tissue and are essential for repair. They are also necessary for the production of haemoglobin, enzymes and hormones. Proteins are also potential sources of energy but are not used if fats and carbohydrates are in plentiful supply.

Protein should account for approximately 15 per cent of total calorie intake. If protein is taken excessively then there are some health risks; for example, kidney damage due to excreting so many unused amino acids.

Examples of sources of protein:

- Meat, fish and poultry are the three primary complete proteins.
- Vegetables and grains are called incomplete proteins because they do not supply all the essential amino acids.

PRACTICAL APPLICATIONS

Protein breaks down more readily during and immediately after exercise. The amount of protein broken down depends upon how long and how hard you exercise.

Increased protein intake may be important during the early stages of training to support increases in muscle mass and myoglobin.

The following nutrients are essential but only needed in small quantities and are often referred to as **micronutrients.**

Vitamins

Vitamins are non-caloric chemical compounds that are needed by the body in small quantities. They are an essential component of our diet because they are vital in the production of energy, the functioning of our metabolism and the prevention of disease. With the exception of vitamin D, the body cannot produce vitamins. Vitamins A, D, E and K are fat-soluble. Vitamins B and C are water-soluble.

A well-balanced diet will ensure sufficient vitamin intake. Vitamins can be found in fresh fruit and vegetables.

 PRACTICAL APPLICATIONS

To make sure you get enough vitamins from your food:

- Buy good-quality fresh fruit and vegetables.
- Wash/scrub food rather than peeling it because vitamins are often found just below the skin.
- Prepare just before cooking and boil in as little water as possible; steaming or microwave cooking is even better.
- Eat soon after cooking.

Extremely large doses of vitamins can be dangerous. An overdose of vitamin A can cause hair loss and enlargement of the liver. There is little evidence to suggest that supplementary vitamin pills can enhance performance and most excess vitamins are simply excreted via urine.

Minerals

These are also non-caloric and are inorganic elements essential for our health. There are two types:

- macro-minerals – needed in large amounts, e.g. calcium, potassium and sodium
- trace elements – needed in very small amounts, e.g. iron, zinc and manganese.

Minerals can be lost through sweating and so there are implications for those who exercise. Minerals should be replaced quickly to ensure good health.

Some important minerals are listed below.

Iron

This is an essential component of haemoglobin, which carries oxygen in the blood. Iron-deficiency anaemia can impair performance in endurance events.

 PRACTICAL APPLICATIONS

In the UK, it has been found that approximately 30% of adult women and 40% of adolescent women are iron deficient. Studies of athletes report higher frequencies of iron problems – research indicates that up to 19% of swimmers and runners may be troubled by iron-deficiences anaemia, which can have a negative impact on performance. Clearly, some people should seek iron-rich foods in their diets. Only a qualified medical doctor should prescribe iron supplements because too much iron can be dangerous. Iron can be found in meat, fish, dairy produce and vegetables. Main sources are red meat and offal.

Calcium

This mineral is essential for healthy bones and teeth. If there is deficiency in calcium, then there is an increased likelihood of osteoporosis and bone fractures. For calcium to be absorbed, there needs to be sufficient vitamin D, which is found in sunlight.

Calcium is found in milk and dairy products, green vegetables and nuts.

PRACTICAL APPLICATIONS

CALCIUM DEFICIENCY
Calcium deficiency can be found in females who are underweight, smokers, alcoholics, vegetarians and those who overdo training and exercise.

Water

This is also a nutrient and is crucial for good health, particularly for those who participate in sport. It carries nutrients in the body and helps with the removal of waste products. It is also very important in the regulation of body temperature. The body loses water through urine and sweat. This water loss accelerates depending on the environment and the duration and intensity of any exercise.

On average, individual daily consumption of water should be about two litres. Those involved in exercise should take more to ensure a good state of hydration. Studies show that individuals who are dehydrated become intolerant to exercise and heat stress. The cardiovascular system becomes inefficient if there is dehydration and there is an inability to provide adequate blood flow to the skin, which may lead to heat exhaustion. Fluids must be taken in during prolonged exercise. This will minimise dehydration and slow the rise in body temperature.

 PRACTICAL APPLICATIONS

There are a number of commercially available sports drinks containing electrolytes and carbohydrates. Some of the claims that are made about these drinks have been misinterpreted. A single balanced meal following exercise can replace all the minerals lost during exercise without the need to consume specialist drinks or supplements. Water is the primary need in any drink taken before, during and after exercise because it empties from the stomach extremely quickly and reduces dehydration associated with sweating. Thirst is not a reliable indicator for fluid intake; therefore it is best to drink small amounts regularly even if you are not thirsty. Under cooler conditions, a carbohydrate drink may give the extra energy needed in events or periods of exercise lasting over an hour.

Fibre

There are two types of dietary fibre soluble and insoluble. There are no calories, vitamins or minerals in fibre and it is not digested when we eat it. Fibre is only found in the cell walls of plants. Foods such as meat, fish and dairy products contain no fibre at all. Fibre is essential for healthy bowel function. When fibre passes through the bowel it absorbs a lot of water, so it increases the bulk of the waste matter. This also makes the waste softer and increases the speed and ease with which it passes through the bowel.

Fibre reduces the risk of a number of bowel problems. These include constipation, haemorrhoids (piles), and cancer of the colon or large bowel.

In the UK most people do not eat enough fibre. Most eat on average about 12g a day or less. Ideally, you should aim for an intake or around 18g a day.

Composition of a healthy diet

Healthy eating involves a daily calorie intake in approximately the following proportions:

- 50 per cent carbohydrate
- 30–35 per cent fat
- 15–20 per cent protein

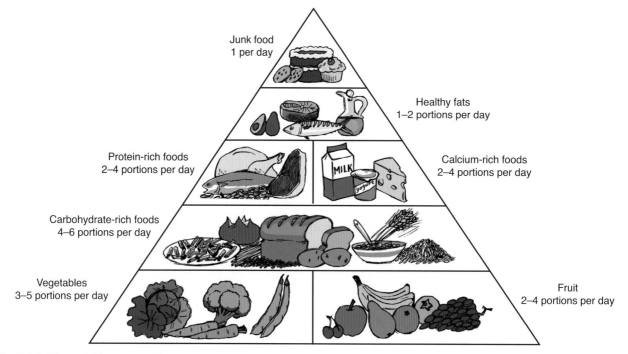

Fig 6.1.2 The nutrition pyramid

When planning your diet, take the following into consideration:

- Food is meant to be enjoyed.
- Make sure you don't have too much fat.
- Avoid too many sugary foods.
- Include vitamins and minerals.
- Eat plenty of fibre.
- Keep alcohol within prescribed limits.
- Maintain a balance of intake and output.
- Eat plenty of fruit and vegetables.

PRACTICAL APPLICATIONS

Alcohol is a concentrated source of energy but cannot be available during exercise for our working muscles.

The Health Development Agency and the National Institute for Health and Clinical Excellence recommend for adults:

- males – 3-4 units per day
- females – 2-3 units per day.

Most advisers agree that 'binge drinking' is particularly bad for you, which is a growing habit amongst teenagers and young adults.

If you are of the legal age to drink it is better to spread your alcohol consumption across the week and to leave some alcohol-free days.

One unit: half pint 'ordinary strength' beer = 3.0-3.5% alcohol = 90 calories;
1 standard glass of wine = 11% alcohol = 90 calories;
single measure spirits = 38% alcohol = 50 calories.

Many believe that there are no healthy or unhealthy foods; there are only bad uses of food. The right balance in a diet is essential for health and fitness. Enjoyment is an important aspect of eating; a healthy diet does not mean that you have to give up all your favourite 'bad' foods – it is the overall balance that counts. Balanced meals contain starchy foods with plenty of vegetables, salad and fruit. Your fat content should be kept to a minimum by using low-fat or lean ingredients.

Factors that also affect choice of foods include:

- culture, morals, ethics
- family influences
- peer-group influences
- lifestyle
- finance.

Eating sufficient fruit and vegetables is important for a healthy diet. It helps to reduce the likelihood of coronary heart disease and some cancers. Government guidelines suggest that you should eat at least five portions of fruit and vegetables each day. This is not a scientifically proven formula but it gives us useful guidance about what are roughly the right levels of intake.

PRACTICAL APPLICATIONS

What is a portion of fruit or vegetables?

2 tablespoons of vegetables	1 cupful of grapes/cherries
1 dessert bowlful of salad	2 tablespoons of fresh fruit salad
1 apple/orange/banana	1 tablespoon dried fruit
2 plums	1 glass fruit juice

Most healthy eating guidelines warn against eating too much salt. If your diet contains too much salt then this may lead to high blood pressure, which can cause heart and kidney disease.

The National Institute for Health and Clinical Excellence (NICE) recommends eating a healthy diet, which means you and your family should:

- base your meals on starchy foods such as potatoes, bread, rice and pasta, choosing wholegrain where possible
- eat plenty of fibre-rich foods such as oats, beans, peas, lentils, grains, seeds, fruit and vegetables, as well as wholegrain bread, and brown rice and pasta
- eat at least five portions of a variety of fruit and vegetables a day in place of foods higher in fat and calories
- avoid foods containing a lot of fat and sugar, such as fried food, sweetened drinks, sweets and chocolate (some takeaways and 'fast' foods contain a lot of fat and sugar)
- eat breakfast
- watch the portion sizes of meals and snacks, and how often you are eating
- avoid taking in too many calories from alcohol.

Active lifestyle

NICE also recommends that small everyday, changes to your activity levels can make a real difference to your health. You don't have to join a gym or sports club (although it can help). For example, you can:

- try walking or cycling to the shops
- avoid sitting for too long in front of the television, at a computer or playing video games (you could try gradually reducing how long you sit down in front of a screen by setting some time limits).

Adults could try to build physical activity into the working day, for example, by taking the stairs instead of the lift, or going for a walk at lunchtime.

Parents can help their children maintain a healthy weight, for instance by playing games that involve moving around a lot like skipping, dancing, running or ball games.

Families should also try to be more active, by walking or cycling to school and the shops, or going swimming or to the local park together.

Source: The National Institute for Health and Clinical Excellence (2008)

Whether or not you participate in regular exercise or sport, you need to eat enough to provide sufficient energy. The body's **metabolism** is often referred to in connection with this. The **basal metabolic rate** (BMR) is a measure of the amount of energy we need at rest. Therefore our food intake needs to take into account our BMR in addition to the energy we require to participate in sport.

Energy is measured in kilocalories and kilojoules. 1KCal = 4.2KJ. Men can consume 2,800-3,000 KCal a day and women 2,000-2,200 KCal a day without putting on weight. However, metabolic rates vary between individuals and your metabolism gets slower as you get older.

Factors that affect energy expenditure:

- frequency of exercise
- intensity of exercise
- type and duration of exercise
- age, gender and body composition of individual
- fuels available.

Fig 6.1.3 Running can be a cheap and effective way to get exercise

The intensity of exercise dictates the use of energy by the muscles. This energy needs to be replaced because otherwise the muscles would not be able to continue to function and the exercise would have to terminate.

There are some effective nutritional strategies for those who exercise regularly.

Glycogen stores

Ensuring that the body has enough glycogen is crucial for optimum energy supply. One method of increasing the glycogen available is through glycogen 'loading', sometimes known as **carbo-loading.** This process involves the sports person depleting their stores of glycogen by cutting down on carbohydrates and keeping to a diet of protein and fat for three days. Light training follows, with a high carbohydrate diet for three days leading up to the event. This has been shown to significantly increase the stores of glycogen and helps to offset fatigue. When carbo-loading the diet should consist mainly of foods like pasta, bread, rice and fruit. Generally a high carbohydrate diet will ensure that glycogen will be replenished during exercise.

Other energy-giving strategies:

- Consume carbohydrates 2–4 hours before exercise.
- Consume a small amount of carbohydrates within the first ½ an hour of exercise to ensure refuelling of glycogen.
- Eat carbohydrates straight after exercise for up to two days to replenish stores.

Fluids

Fig 6.1.4 Rehydration is essential during a match

You can lose up to one litre of water per hour during endurance exercise; therefore rehydration is essential, especially if there are also hot environmental conditions. As we have discovered, thirst is not a good indicator of dehydration, therefore the athlete needs to drink plenty during and after exercise even if they don't feel thirsty.

PRACTICAL APPLICATIONS

TAKING FLUIDS

Take fluids, preferably water before exercise to ensure full hydration.
Take fluids continuously during exercise even if not thirsty.
Small amounts often is best.

Take fluids straight after exercise before alcohol is consumed.
Some sports-specific drinks may be useful for high-intensity and long-duration exercise.

Vitamin and mineral supplements

There is an increase in the body's requirements for vitamins and minerals if regular, intensive exercise takes place. This means that the athlete will eat more food because of the need for more energy. This in itself will mean that the body is receiving more vitamins and minerals. As we have already seen, large quantities of extra vitamins and minerals can damage health. However, supplementing the athlete's diet can in certain circumstances be beneficial.

 PRACTICAL APPLICATIONS

SUPPLEMENTS

(Please note that supplementation is best undertaken with medical supervision.)
Smokers should consider extra vitamin C.
If planning to become pregnant it is recommended that folic acid is taken.

If you are on a diet and consuming less than 1,200 calories per day, supplements in low doses have been found to be beneficial.
If you are vegan or vegetarian and your diet is limited, multi-vitamins and mineral supplements could be useful.

Factors to consider with sports performers and nutrition

Sports performers, especially at the top level, have certain aspects to their lifestyles that should be considered when planning nutritional intake:

- timing of meals to fit around training and events
- ensuring that there is balance in the diet
- ensuring adequate fluid intake
- ensuring adequate iron intake
- diet should be suitable for very high workload, depending on the activity
- psychological well-being – if an athlete is unhappy with the diet, then even if physiologically beneficial, it could negatively affect performance because of psychological pressure
- there should be a sharing of ideas between coach/dietician and performer to agree the best strategy, depending on an individual's needs and perceptions
- obsession with food is common with high-performance athletes and should be avoided.

 ACTIVITY 2

TASK

Collect information about your diet.
Keep a food diary or logbook, detailing what you eat each day over a one- or two-week period.
Write a report and identify the strengths of your diet, e.g. good water intake, and its weaknesses, e.g. levels of fat too high.

CHALLENGE
Identify what you would do to improve your diet, e.g. eat more fruit and vegetables, eat at different times of the day or drink more fluid.
   Justify your choice of diet by giving reasons for food and fluid choices.

Plan your diet

Your nutritional strategy or your future diet should take into account the essential food groups we have identified.

* Ensure that you have the right balance of foods.
* Ensure regular rehydration.
* Take into account the way you cook food – e.g. overboiling vegetables destroys all-important vitamins.
* Take into account the timing of your eating.
* Review whether it is necessary to take supplements such as vitamins, minerals, creatine and protein powders.
* Please note that any significant change in your diet or any use of nutritional supplements must be approved by a qualified nutritionist or doctor.

THE EFFECTS OF FACTORS SUCH AS AGE, GENDER AND DISABILITY ON PARTICIPATION AND PERFORMANCE IN PHYSICAL ACTIVITY

There are many reasons for participation and non-participation in an active healthy lifestyle. The following are some of the most relevant.

Time

Many people decide not to participate in sport because of work or other commitments. It is common to hear the phrase 'I haven't got the time'. This is legitimate, but a person's perception of how much time is available is often different to reality; for example, getting home from work and watching television all evening is a way of spending leisure time, and people who do this are choosing to spend their leisure time in a passive rather than an active way.

Resources

Depending on where you live, you may or may not have facilities or sports clubs near to you. This has an obvious effect on whether or not you participate in sport. One way of increasing participation for those who do not have facilities close by would be a transport service readily available for those who wish to visit a sports facility.

Fitness/ability

Some people do not join in with sports activities because they perceive that they are not good enough. This perception may well have arisen from previous experiences, e.g. at school. They may have failed in an activity and felt humiliated and therefore feel that they are a hopeless case.

To get rid of this feeling of hopelessness, it is important that such an individual experiences success in some aspect of sport so that they regain their confidence. After all, it is extremely unlikely that there is no sport out there that a particular individual cannot even be remotely good at!

The examiner may ask you to explain the effects of these factors. Make sure you give reasons in your explanation – remember it is difficult not to explain if you use the word 'because'!

Health problems

There are genuine health reasons for some people not to participate in sport, although many medical practitioners encourage an active lifestyle as part of prevention and treatment plans. Most rehabilitation regimes include physical exercise and what better way to exercise than sport? Obesity is on the increase in the western world due to our diets and lack of exercise, but weight-related embarrassment prevents many people taking the first step towards sport. There needs to be encouragement and the right environment for such people to get involved in physical activity. Clubs such as 'weight watchers' can play a positive role here, although some people feel that joining such an organisation is demeaning and only reinforces low self-esteem. Lack of self-esteem is an important factor and must be tackled in order for an individual to gain the confidence to participate in sport.

Access

The growth of sports facilities has increased access but although there are more low-cost courses available, some people still cannot afford to participate in sport. For many the most important questions relating to access are: what is available; what is affordable; will I fit in?

The following are the main issues related to access:

- opening times – e.g. may not be convenient for shift workers
- age – e.g. sport often perceived as a 'young person's activity' and the elderly may feel undignified if they participate in sport
- race – e.g. experiencing racial discrimination may be one reason for a lack of confidence to get involved in a predominantly white environment such as a golf club
- disability – e.g. lack of suitable facilities, such as no wheelchair ramp or doors that are too narrow.

 PRACTICAL APPLICATIONS

In one UK city, the participants' ethnic origin is a huge influence on the types of sports chosen. For example, just 2 per cent of Pakistani residents go swimming, compared with 36 per cent of white and Indian people.

The average life expectancy has increased and so there are increasing numbers of older people who could take advantage of opportunities for physical activity. There are more veterans' teams in a variety of sports and there is a growing awareness that activity in old age can enrich the quality of life experiences.

Those with disabilities now have much better access to physical activities. Disability sport is recognised as a sport in its own right, with UK participants who have achieved great success in international competition.

The media has also played its part in changing the nature of exercise in the UK. There is an increase in high technology that brings sporting events from around the world live into our living rooms every day. Sport, exercise and healthy living are often headline news, with documentaries, films and promotion of products associated with active, healthy lifestyles. This all raises the profile of physical activity, and the interest and enthusiasm for an active, healthy lifestyle is fed and reinforced by the media.

Fig 6.1.5 Age is no barrier to exercise, nor is disability

PRACTICAL APPLICATIONS

Sporting Equals is a national initiative working to promote racial equality in sport throughout England. It is a partnership between Sport England and the Commission for Racial Equality. Ethnic minorities are poorly represented at decision-making levels in most sports. They are largely excluded from various sports facilities, and are overlooked by sports development officers and coaches.

Sporting Equals works with the governing bodies of various sports and with national organisations to develop policies and working practices that promote racial equality.

LIFESTYLE-RELATED FACTORS AFFECTING HEALTH

Our lifestyle (the way in which we conduct our everyday lives) can significantly affect our overall fitness and health. Many of us now live in a less active way. There is an increase in people being overweight or extremely overweight (obese). There are more instances of diabetes and coronary heart disease, which is affected by the food we eat.

The main 'lifestyle' factors that can affect our physical fitness are:

- stress levels – there is now an increase in stress-related ailments, often due to our hectic lives that leave little room for relaxation. Modern life is very competitive, and, for many, getting involved in physical activity is a low priority. Others, however, find that active hobbies are a great release from everyday life and find participating in sport relaxing
- alcohol, smoking and drugs.

Smoking

Few people who are serious about an active, healthy lifestyle smoke. There is overwhelming evidence that health and fitness is affected adversely by smoking, whatever age you are. Cigarettes contain tar, nicotine, carbon monoxide and other irritants that cause coughing. Normally haemoglobin in the blood carries oxygen. However, when carbon monoxide is present in the body, haemoglobin seems to prefer this and once it has taken up carbon monoxide it is unable to take up oxygen again, so less oxygen circulates in the bloodstream. Up to 10 per cent of the oxygen-carrying capacity can be lost in this way.

PRACTICAL APPLICATIONS

SMOKING AND PHYSICAL ACTIVITY
The time it takes to complete physical activities is increased after smoking.
  Endurance and capacity for exercise are reduced in proportion to the cigarettes smoked – the more you smoke, the less fit you will be.

Training has less effect on smokers – so you can train or exercise really hard but smoking can undo all the good work.

Smoking is the biggest cause of preventable death in the western world. It kills more than 120,000 people in the UK every year, with most dying from three main diseases: cancer, chronic obstructive lung disease (bronchitis and emphysema) and coronary heart disease. Around 29 per cent of men and 25 per cent of women in the UK smoke. However, these figures are an average for the population as a whole; the figures for those on low incomes and from poor backgrounds are much higher. One in two regular cigarette smokers will probably be killed by their habit.

Drugs

The use of drugs, whether they be recreational (e.g. cannabis) or performance enhancing (e.g. anabolic steroids), is widespread and can seriously affect your health and well-being.

Drug taking involves the use of chemicals that alter the way we feel and see things and is one of the oldest activities of the human race.

Even when there are serious consequences from using drugs, those consequences will not always be enough to stop people. If and when they do decide to give up, they may find that it is harder than they thought.

There is often more to an addiction than the physical withdrawal symptoms. Addiction includes anxiety, depression and lowering of self-esteem. The pattern of these symptoms will depend not only on the drug used, but also on the psychological make-up of the person and the circumstances in which they are attempting to remain drug-free.

www.uksport.gov.uk
More information about anti-doping and testing.

www.100percentme.co.uk
Promotes drug-free sport and gives invaluable information for sports participants regarding the use of medication and what you can and cannot take as a medicine.

The issue of doping in sport is a key concern and UK Sport has been designated by government to deliver its policy objectives as the national anti-doping organisation, to represent government in international meetings and to co-ordinate the national anti-doping programme of testing, education and information for sport throughout the UK. There are three widely known substances or methods used for blood doping (the boosting of red blood cells in the circulation to improve athletic performance):

- the use of ergthropoietin (EPO)
- the use of synthetic oxygen carriers, and
- blood transfusions.

Anti-doping involves tests that can reveal whether illegal methods have been used to increase the number of oxygen-carrying red blood cells.

Athletes are advised to check all medications and substances with their doctor or governing body medical officer. All substances should be checked carefully when travelling abroad as many products can, and do, contain different substances to those found in the UK.

PRACTICAL APPLICATIONS

Prohibited substances may vary from sport to sport. It is the athlete's responsibility to know their sport's anti-doping regulations. In cases of uncertainty, it is important to check with the appropriate governing body or UK Sport and be sure to read carefully the anti-doping rules adopted by the relevant governing body and international sports federations.

Certain substances and practices are prohibited in sport for various reasons including:

- performance-enhancing effects, which contravene the ethics of sport and undermine the principles of fair participation
- health and safety of the athlete – some drug misuse may cause serious side effects, which can compromise an athlete's health. Using substances to mask pain/injury could make an injury worse or cause permanent damage. Some drug misuse may be harmful to other athletes participating in the sport.
- illegality – it is forbidden by law to possess or supply some substances.

Most sporting federations have anti-doping regulations to ensure all athletes abide by the same principle of being drug-free. The regulations aim to achieve drug-free sport through clearly stated policies, testing and sanctions. They are also intended to raise the awareness of drug misuse and to deter athletes from using prohibited drugs and engaging in prohibited practices.

Prohibited classes of substances include:

- stimulants
- narcotic analgesics
- anabolic agents
- anabolic androgenic steroids (see Chapter 6.2 for more on these)
- other anabolic agents
- diuretics
- peptide hormones, mimetics and analogues
- substances with anti-oestrogenic activity
- masking agents (substances that can mask illegal, performance-enhancing drugs)

Prohibited practices include:

- enhancement of oxygen transfer
- blood doping
- administration of products that enhance the uptake, transport and delivery of oxygen
- pharmacological, chemical and physical manipulation
- gene doping.

In certain circumstances, the following classes of substances are also prohibited:

- alcohol
- cannabinoids
- local anaesthetics
- glucocorticosteroids
- beta-blockers.

Other lifestyle factors

There are other lifestyle factors that affect your fitness levels.

Sleep

The amount of sleep you get can affect the way you feel as well as your sports performance. It is important to get enough sleep. People sleep anywhere between

5 and 11 hours, with the average being 7.75 hours. It is generally accepted that the amount of sleep we require is that which stops us being sleepy during the day.

Job

Your health and physical fitness are also affected by the type of job you have. Some people have jobs that involve sitting at a desk all day – this is known as a **sedentary** type of work. Others who have active jobs may be more physically fit even before training for sport.

METHODS OF EXERCISE FOR AN ACTIVE, HEALTHY LIFESTYLE

The methods we can choose for an active, healthy lifestyle are numerous and it is beyond the scope of this book to cover all of them. They include the activities you will have chosen for the practical component of the GCSE in Physical Education. If you participate in a physical activity you may well do other types of exercise to get fit enough for that activity – for instance, a training programme or a general fitness routine.

The ways in which exercise and training programmes can enable you to get fit and healthy will be dealt with later in this book. The following are some general descriptions of exercise methods identified in the GCSE PE specification.

Circuit training

This involves a series of exercises called a **circuit** because the training involves repetition of each activity. The resistance that is used in circuits relates mainly to body weight and each exercise in the circuit is designed to work on a particular muscle group. In order to train effectively different muscle groups should be worked on, with no two muscle-groups being worked on one after the other; for instance, an activity that uses the main muscle groups in the arms should then be followed by an exercise involving a different muscle group such as the legs.

The types of exercises that are involved in circuit training are: press-ups, star jumps, dips and squat thrusts.

Circuit training can also incorporate skills; for example, hockey players may include dribbling activities, flicking the ball, shuttle runs and shooting activities.

 The examiner will ask for a description of the following methods and a brief explanation of how they help in health and fitness.

The duration and intensity of circuit training depends on the type of activities that have been used. An example would be a circuit with 1 minute's worth of activity, followed by 1 minute's worth of rest. The whole circuit could then be repeated three times. Scores at the end of the circuit may be related to time or repetitions and are a good way of motivating in training. It is also easy to see progression in fitness as the weeks go by when more repetitions can be attempted or times are improved.

Aerobics including body pump, spin and dance exercise

These are all types of cardiovascular exercise and involve sustained, rhythmic activity using large muscle groups. Aerobic exercise also makes the lungs work harder as the body's need for oxygen is increased.

There are numerous benefits for health and general well-being to be gained from regular cardiovascular exercise:

- increased energy levels
- reduced stress and improved mental health (due to the release of endorphins in the brain)
- increased heart and lung efficiency
- reduced blood pressure, resting heart rate and risk of stroke or heart attack.

The local gym will provide a wide variety of aerobic options, such as treadmills, cross trainers, exercise bikes, stairmasters, rowing machines and ski machines. It is a good idea to use different machines, speeds and levels of resistance as your body can get used to a certain routine and you may also get bored!

If you prefer to work out with others, many gyms and leisure centres provide classes, such as various forms of dance, body pump, body combat and step aerobics with a trained instructor. Always check that the instructor is suitably qualified.

Swimming is also a very effective cardiovascular activity. As it is very low impact it is often suitable for people who have had injuries or problems with muscles or joints.

 PRACTICAL APPLICATIONS

For good cardiovascular fitness it is generally recommended to exercise 3 to 5 times a week and for 30–60 minutes, not including warming up at the start and cooling down at the end.

The main thing is to ensure that your heart and lungs are worked hard enough and for long enough to gain the benefits of aerobic exercise but not so long that you run the risk of injury. To check whether you are working out at the correct intensity, you should be out of breath but still capable of speaking.

If a half-hour session feels like too much, start with 10 minute sessions for the first week then increase that to 15 or 20 minute sessions the next week and so on until you feel comfortable exercising for longer. If your joints start to feel sore or breathing becomes uncomfortable, slow down or stop to ensure that you are in a fit state for your next session.

Aqua aerobics

This, as the name suggests, is aerobic exercise in the water. It normally takes place in shallow water at a swimming pool and as part of an organised group session that can last anywhere between 30 minutes and an hour. Workouts usually comprise routines familiar to those who have experienced land aerobics, and could include jumping jacks, cross-country skiing motion and walking and running backwards and forwards.

The support the water provides for the body greatly reduces the risk of bone, muscle and joint injury, its density meaning that 90 per cent of a body's weight is supported.

Exercising in the water is also a great way to relieve stress, as the water massages and cools the body, relaxing the participant as they exercise.

Aqua aerobics is a good activity for those wanting to improve the health of their heart and lungs and burn some calories without too much risk of injury.

Yoga

Yoga was developed by the ancient wise men of India and is a system of personal development involving body, mind and spirit that dates back more than 5,000 years. The aim of this integrated approach of mind and body control is ultimate physical health and happiness, together with mental peace and tranquillity.

Today, yoga is practised for general health, and for its preventive and curative effects.

There are various types of yoga, all of them leading ultimately to the same goal – unification with the Divine. The yoga paths can be broadly classified into:

- Bhakti yoga: Path of Devotion
- Karma yoga: Path of Selfless Action
- Jnana yoga: Path of Transcendental Knowledge
- Ashtanga yoga: Path of Patanjali (eight-step path).

In the western world yoga is recognised mainly as Hatha yoga, which is a combination of Asanas (physical exercises and postures), Pranayama (breathing techniques) and meditation. Hatha yoga is said to provide a balanced and wholesome approach to achieving perfect physical and mental health, happiness and tranquillity.

Eastern yogis believe that asanas are simply a stepping stone to higher paths and that working only on the body is a waste of time as the body is mortal whereas the soul is immortal. Hatha yoga is in fact a single step in the eight-step path of Ashtanga yoga.

Many people learn yoga by attending classes; however, videos and books teaching yoga are also popular. As with all exercises, technique is very important and for this reason it is advisable for beginners to seek out a reputable teacher.

Yoga can be practised by anyone, at any age. It develops flexibility and muscular endurance and, like many of the martial arts, incorporates techniques to relieve stress and bring the mind and body into harmony. Yoga, a Sanskrit word for 'union', means an experience of oneness or union with your inner being (self).

Continuous traning

Continuous training is a method that involves few if any rest intervals and carries on for a long period of time, normally at a low level of intensity or not very fast. This type of training improves stamina or endurance and is therefore mostly aerobic exercise.

Pilates

Pilates is an exercise method developed by its founder Joseph Pilates to try to improve physical and mental health. Pilates focuses on building your body's core strength and improving your posture through a series of low-repetition, low-impact stretching and conditioning exercises.

Fig 6.1.6 Yoga is good for general fitness

www.bwy.org.uk
The British Wheel of Yoga's site contains more details about the practise and teaching of yoga.

www.yogauk.com
A useful site that provides information about yoga teachers and different types of yoga.

www.pilatesfoundation.co.uk
For more information about pilates and how to practise it safely and effectively.

Through pilates, you may be able to develop the core muscles without adding bulk, increasing your flexibility and agility and toning your stomach and thigh muscles.

Pilates is based on eight principles:

- relaxation
- alignment
- control
- precision
- routine
- breathing
- centring
- flowing movement.

 PRACTICAL APPLICATIONS

CORE STABILITY TRAINING
The main aim of core training or core stability training is to exercise the trunk muscles but control your lumbar spine position during exercise. Core stability training involves performing exercises for your abdominals and lower back. These muscles are involved in a major way in any sport and so it is very important to maintain and develop their strength.

Core strength
By core strength, we mean strength in your back, abdominal and pelvic muscles.

Strengthening the core area should be part all training programmes. It involves a variety of abdominal and lower back exercises performed three or four times a week. There are weight or resistance machines that will strengthen the muscles of the abdomen and lower back, exercises on mats, and the use of a large inflated ball called a 'Swiss ball'.

 PRACTICAL APPLICATIONS

CORE STABILITY EXERCISES
The 'plank': Lie on the floor face down. Hold a straight body position, supported on elbows and toes. Brace the abdominals and set the lower back in a neutral position. Hold this position for an increasing length of time up to a maximum of one minute. Perform two to three sets.

The 'side plank': Lie on one side, ensuring the top hip is above the bottom hip. Push up until there is a straight bodyline through feet, hips and head. Keep the elbow under the shoulder. Lower under control and repeat on opposite side. Hold this position for an increasing length of time up to a maximum of one minute. Perform two to three sets.

 REVIEW QUESTIONS

1 What are the main characteristics of a balanced, healthy lifestyle?
2 Identify and describe three indicators of health and well-being.
3 What are the main components of a healthy diet?
4 What effects does a healthy diet have on the body?
5 Describe the effects of age on participation and performance in physical activity.
6 What are the main effects of smoking on performance and participation in physical activity?
7 What are the problems with performance-enhancing drugs?
8 Which group of people are most involved in physical activity in the UK? (Refer to age and gender in your answer.)
9 What are the main types of physical activity that are popular in the UK?
10 Describe one method of exercise, other than a sport, for an active, healthy lifestyle.

EXAM-STYLE QUESTIONS

Multiple choice questions:

1 One of the factors that do NOT affect participation in an active, healthy lifestyle is:
   a age
   b gender
   c reaction time
   d smoking.

2 The following are both examples of carbohydrates:
   a cheese and fish
   b bananas and bread
   c cereal and meat
   d eggs and mushrooms.

3 After an hour's vigorous exercise programme, a 16-year-old male, who does not train regularly, experiences some short-term effects on his body. Which one of the following would you NOT expect to happen after such a short exercise programme:
   a increase in sweating
   b high heart rate
   c increase in lung volume
   d increased breathing rate?

4 Participation in physical activities can lead to many health benefits. Which of the following is a direct health benefit?
   a learn new movement skills in sport
   b make friends
   c manage stress more easily
   d raise confidence.

Short answer questions

1 Briefly describe the long-term effects of exercise on the heart.   **(3 marks)**
2 Describe the main characteristics of a balanced, healthy lifestyle. **(5 marks)**
3 Identify and describe three indicators of health and well-being.   **(3 marks)**
4 What are the main effects of alcohol on performance and participation in physical activity?   **(4 marks)**
5 Describe a method of exercise that you may participate in to be more active and healthy. Explain its positive effects.   **(4 marks)**

WHAT YOU NEED TO KNOW

- the characteristics of a balanced, healthy lifestyle (SC)
- the main indicators of health and well-being (SC)
- the components of a healthy diet (SC)
- the functions of a healthy diet (SC)
- the effects of age, gender and disability on participation and performance in physical activity (SC)
- the effects of smoking, alcohol, diet and performance-enhancing drugs on performance and participation in physical activity (SC)
- the levels of participation in physical activity in the UK (SC)
- the methods of exercise for an active, healthy lifestyle (e.g. circuit training/ aerobics/pilates/yoga). (SC)

6.2 HEALTHY, ACTIVE LIFESTYLES IN PRACTICE

LEARNING GOALS

By the end of this section you should be able to:

- describe and explain the short-term and long-term effects of an active lifestyle
- identify and describe training principles of overload, specificity, progression and reversibility
- apply these principles in planning a targeted exercise or training programme
- identify and describe the FITT principle
- give a simple description of aerobic and anaerobic exercise
- identify potential hazards with practical examples in a range of physical activity settings
- explain how to minimise risks in a range of physical activity settings
- explain the importance of personal hygiene in physical activity.

> The main short-term effects can be listed and learned for the examination. These can often give valuable marks.
>
> Short-term effects of exercise on the respiratory system:
> - breathing rate increases
> - tidal volume increases
> - minute volume increaes.
>
> Short-term effects on the heart:
> - heart rate increases
> - cardiac output increases
> - stroke volume increases.
>
> Short-term effects on muscles:
> - muscle tiredness/fatigue
> - increase in temperature of muscles.
>
> The examiner will not be asking any detailed questions about volumes but *will* ask how these are affected by exercise, both in the short term and the long term.

EFFECTS OF A BALANCED, HEALTHY LIFESTYLE ON THE CARDIOVASCULAR, RESPIRATORY AND MUSCULAR SYSTEMS

Cardiovascular system

Short-term effects

The following are short-term responses relating to the cardiovascular system.

There is a rise in heart rate which is designed to get the body ready for activity – called an 'anticipatory rise'. This is due to hormonal action; stimulation from the sense organs causes a sharp rise in the levels of certain hormones. The heart rate continues high due to physical exertion, then remains steady for a period and finally falls due to the withdrawal of stimuli and the drop in hormone levels. Eventually the heart rate returns to its resting rate.

Respiratory system

Tidal volume (TV) This is the volume of air either inspired or expired per breath. This increases during exercise.

Inspiratory reserve volume (IRV) This is the maximal volume inspired in addition to the tidal volume. This decreases during exercise.

Expiratory reserve volume (ERV) This is the maximal volume expired in addition to the tidal volume. This decreases slightly during exercise.

Residual volume (RV) This is the amount of air left in the lungs after maximal expiration. This slightly increases during exercise.

Total lung capacity (TLC) This is the vital capacity plus the residual volume and is the volume at the end of maximal inspiration. This slightly decreases during exercise.

Vital capacity (VC) This is the maximum amount of air that can be forcibly exhaled after maximal inspiration. This slightly decreases during exercise.

Breathing rate This increases due to demands for more oxygen.

Overall long-term effects

- Increase in bone density. This strengthens bones and makes them more healthy.
- Increase in capillary density and efficiency, enabling capillaries to provide us with more energy throughout the day.
- Lower resting heart rate. This enables us to do more each day and to exercise longer and harder.
- Increased vital capacity. This enables us to uptake more oxygen, which again increases our energy levels throughout the day.
- Increase in stroke volume at rest and during exercise. This enables more oxygen to be used by our working muscles and organs.
- Cardiac output increases. This again will enable us to be more energetic and healthy.
- Decrease in resting blood pressure, which will help to offset disease and keep us healthy.
- Increase in haemoglobin, which helps carry oxygen, along with increase in red blood cells. The more oxygen that is available, the more work we can carry out and for longer.
- You are able to work harder and longer.

Effects of exercise on the muscular system

The following are the long-term adaptations of the muscular system after a period of exercise and following an active, healthy balanced lifestyle.

Aerobic adaptations in muscle. Activities like swimming or running can enlarge slow-twitch fibres, which gives greater potential for energy production.

Size and number of mitochondria increased, again giving us more energy.

Increase in **myoglobin** content within the muscle cell, enabling more oxygen to be used by our working muscles.

Onset of fatigue delayed because of higher maximum oxygen uptake (VO_2 max.). This will enable us to work harder and for longer and not to tire too quickly.

Anaerobic adaptations in muscle. Activities like sprinting or weight lifting can cause hypertrophy of fast-twitch muscle fibres. This will strengthen our muscles and make them more efficient.

Size of heart increases – called **cardiac hypertrophy**. This will make our heart healthier and ward off the onset of heart disease.

PRACTICAL APPLICATIONS

With a healthy lifestyle muscles can keep going on the repetitive tasks that are involved in everyday life, work, sport and exercise; for example, healthy muscles help you finish an exercise routine or keep up with your friends when walking home from school.

The examiner will be looking for you to be able to name each principle and explain how it can be used to improve fitness.

TRAINING PRINCIPLES OF OVERLOAD, SPECIFICITY, PROGRESSION AND REVERSIBILITY

A training programme should take into account differences between individuals. An individual's goals must be understood; for example, does the performer want to get generally fit or fit for a particular sport? The individual's current activity level must be assessed and initial fitness testing may be appropriate. The age, time available, equipment available and skill level must all be taken into consideration before the following principles of training are applied.

Specificity

This principle indicates that the training undertaken should be specific and relevant to the needs of the activity or the type of sport involved; for instance, a sprinter would carry out more anaerobic training because the event is mostly anaerobic in nature. It is not just energy systems that have to be specific; muscle groups and actions involved in the training also have to be as specific as possible. There is, however, a consensus that good general fitness is required before any high degree of specificity can be applied.

Overload

This principle underpins the need to work the body harder than normal so that there is some stress and discomfort. Adaptation and progress will follow overload because the body will respond by adapting to the stress experienced; for instance, in weight training the lifter will eventually attempt heavier weights or an increase in repetitions, thus overloading the body. Overload can be achieved by a combination of increasing the frequency, the intensity and the duration of the activity.

Progression

Not only has overload got to occur, but also it should progressively become more difficult. Once adaptations have occurred, then the performer should make even more demands on the body. It is important that progression does not mean 'overdoing it'. Training must be sensibly progressive and realistic if it is to be effective, otherwise injury may occur and there would be regression instead of progression.

Reversibility

This principle states that performance can deteriorate if training stops or decreases in intensity for any length of time. If training is stopped, then the fitness gained will be largely lost. For instance, VO_2 max and muscle strength can decrease.

Variance

This principle states that there should be variety in training methods. If training is too predictable, then performers can become demotivated and bored. Overuse injuries are also common when training is too repetitive with one muscle group or part of the body, so variance can also help prevent injury.

ACTIVITY 3

TASK
Plan an hour of exercise and include the principles of overload and specificity.
CHALLENGE
Plan an outline 6-week programme and justify your activities by referring to all the principles of training listed above.

The specification demands that you know what FITT stands for and that you can give a practical example of each element and how it might affect health and fitness.

THE FITT PRINCIPLE

The 'FITT' method is a way of ensuring that training adheres to the principles of training. FITT stands for:

F = frequency of training (number of training sessions each week). This will depend on the level of ability and fitness of the performer. The elite athlete will train every day, whereas the lower-level club player may train only once per week. The type of training undertaken also dictates the frequency – aerobic training can be followed 5 or 6 times per week. Strength training, however, may only be undertaken 3 or 4 times per week.

 PRACTICAL APPLICATIONS

How frequently you exercise or train depends on your ability and fitness level. You should also bear in mind the progression and overload principles.
Too much training can be as harmful as not enough.

I = intensity of the exercise undertaken. This will again take into account the individual differences of the performer and the type of training being undertaken. A 'training zone' is often created for aerobic training where heart-rate ranges dictate the intensity of training. It is suggested that there should be a training intensity of 60–75 per cent of maximal heart rate reserve for the average athlete.

T = time or duration that the training takes up. If aerobic training is required, this should be a minimum of 20 minutes or so. To be effective the duration of the training must take into account the intensity of training.

T = type of training to fulfil specific needs. The methods of training are described earlier in this chapter and the type of sport (or your role in that sport) will dictate what type of training you follow. A triathlete, for example, will train in all areas of fitness but will pay particular attention to aerobic and muscular endurance because of the nature of the sport. For archery the type of training might include aspects of muscular endurance to keep muscles steady for effective aiming.

PRACTICAL APPLICATIONS

Two days of a week's training programme for a Premiership football player

Monday
rehab work such as massage and physiotherapy
30 minutes own programme of core exercises and warm-up
10 minutes run at moderate pace followed by ballistic stretching
20 minutes interval work with 'ladder' training for quick footwork. 10 sprints followed by stretching
10 minutes 'keep ball' in small grids
10 minutes further grid work inc. 4 v 1 and 3 v 2
20 minutes defenders and attackers separate drills, e.g. forwards shooting drills
30 minutes all involved in link-up play
10 minutes warm-down and further rehab where necessary.

Tuesday
rehab work and physiotherapy where required
30 minutes own programme of core exercises and warm-up including ballistic stretching and ending in short sprints
30 minutes 'keep ball' and 2 teams 9 v 9 possession game with restrictions to improve quick passing and control
30 minutes grid work from 1 v 1 through to 4 v 4
10 minutes 5 a side with two touch restrictions
20 minutes short run intervals with 100 per cent intensity
20 minutes circuit training
10 minutes warm-down
1 hour's rest
10 minutes warm-up
60 minutes weight training for strength and power
10 minutes warm-down and further rehab if necessary.

AEROBIC AND ANAEROBIC TRAINING

Aerobic exercise is physical exercise that improves the efficiency of the cardiovascular system and enables it to carry and use more oxygen.

Aerobic capacity can be improved through continuous, steady state (submaximal) training. The rhythmic exercise classes known as 'aerobics' are the most obvious example but other exercises such as continuous swimming or jogging are also good for aerobic fitness. This low-intensity exercise must take place over a long period of time, from 20 minutes to 2 hours. The intensity of this exercise should be 60–80 per cent of your maximum heart rate.

> The specification demands only simple descriptions of aerobic and anaerobic exercise.

Anaerobic exercise is when the body is working in the absence of oxygen – for example, lifting something quickly off the floor or sprinting for a ball. This type of activity can only be carried out for a short amount of time because it leads to a lack of oxygen and the build-up of lactic acid.

Anaerobic training involves high-intensity work that may be less frequent, although elite athletes will frequently train both aerobically and anaerobically.

TYPES OF EXERCISE

Interval training

This is one of the most popular types of training. It is adaptable depending on individual needs and sports. Interval training can improve both aerobic and anaerobic fitness. It is called interval training because there are intervals of work and intervals of rest. For training the aerobic system, there should be slower intervals, which makes it suitable for sports like athletics and swimming and for team games like hockey or football. For training the anaerobic system, there should be shorter, more intense, intervals of training.

Fartlek training

This is also known as 'speed-play' training. This training is good for aerobic fitness because it is an endurance activity. It is good for anaerobic fitness because of the speed activities over a short period of time. Throughout the exercise, the speed and intensity of the training is varied. In a one-hour session, for instance, there may be a walking activity that is low in intensity to very fast sprinting, which is high intensity. Cross-country running with sprint activities every now and again is a simplistic but reasonable way of describing **fartlek**. Fartlek could also be incorporated into road running and it has the added benefit of being a more varied and enjoyable way of endurance training. It helps to train both the aerobic and the anaerobic energy systems and is ideal for many team sports that include intermittent sprinting and long periods of moderate activity.

Weight and resistance training methods

In circuit training we have seen that it is the body weight that is used as resistance to enable the body to work hard and to physiologically adapt to the training stresses. For strength to be developed, more resistance can be used in the form of weight training or against other types of resistance (such as the use of pulleys). Weight training involves a number of repetitions and sets, depending on the type of strength that needs to be developed. For throwing events in athletics, for example, training methods must involve very high resistance and low repetition.

For strength endurance that you may need in swimming or cycling, more repetitions need to be involved with less resistance or lighter weights.

Plyometrics

This type of training is designed to improve dynamic strength. Plyometrics improves the speed in which muscles shorten. If muscles have previously been stretched, then they tend to generate more force when contracted. Any sport that involves sprinting, throwing and jumping will benefit from this type of training, as will players of many team sports like netball or rugby.

Plyometrics involve bounding, hopping and jumping, when muscles have to work concentrically (jumping up) and eccentrically (landing). One type of jumping used in this training method is called in-depth jumping, which is when the athlete jumps on to and off boxes. This type of training is very strenuous on the muscles and joints and a reasonable amount of fitness must be present before this training is attempted. As usual, it is important that there is sufficient stretching of the muscle before attempting this type of training.

Flexibility training

This is sometimes called mobility training. It involves stretching exercises of the muscles and this can help with performance and to avoid injury. There are two types of flexibility exercises:

- Active stretching
- Passive stretching

This is when there are voluntary muscular contractions that are held by the performer for 30 seconds to one minute. When the muscle is relaxed at the limit of the stretching range, muscle elongation may occur if this practice is repeated regularly. So the more you stretch, the more flexible you will be so long as the stretching is under control and muscles are suitable warmed-up before stretching begins.

One method of active stretching is called the ballistic method. The performer actively uses the momentum of the limb to move the body through a wider range of movement. This is achieved through a bouncing type movement and should only be attempted by those who are extremely flexible, such as gymnasts or certain athletes, because muscle tissue damage is easily experienced with such active stretching.

Passive stretching

This technique incorporates an external 'helper', who pushes or pulls the limb to stretch the appropriate muscles. Obviously, this is potentially dangerous, so the subject must be thoroughly warmed up and should go through some active stretching to begin with. Gymnasts often favour this particular type of stretching. One type of passive stretching is called proprioceptive neuromuscular facilitation (PNF).

THE SAFE AND POSITIVE ENVIRONMENT FOR AN ACTIVE, HEALTHY LIFESTYLE

The main risks and hazards for participants, leaders and officials in physical activities and sport are as follows:

Poor physical fitness/inappropriate physique for the activity

Physical activities require at least some level of fitness of the participant; for example, to be involved in gymnastics you need to have some flexibility and the ability to support your own weight. An exercise class may demand a certain level of fitness in participants if they are to keep going. A netball player needs to have some stamina and the ability to run up and down a netball court. Most physical activities and sports are quite physically demanding and any person who has an injury or health problems should seek advice from a qualified medical practitioner before participating. If you wish to play rugby football as a forward you will need to be physically strong in order to withstand the physical demands of scrimmaging and minimise the risk of injury.

Poor level of skill or technique

Many injuries are caused through inexperience. Some players new to physical activities and sport will not know how to participate safely; for example, in hockey more injuries relating to inappropriate use of the hockey stick are sustained at lower-ability levels – a novice player does not have the stick control of a more experienced player. Club squash player have more eye injuries than international players because the ball is more likely to be struck in an inappropriate or unpredictable manner. Those who participate in physical activities and sports also sustain injuries because of poor technique. A golfer who has an inefficient golf swing can sustain back injuries. A tennis player who uses the wrist too much in shots may suffer wrist sprains. A javelin thrower in athletics who does not throw with a correct technique can suffer arm, leg and back strains.

Lack of effective preparation

It is crucial that all performers in physical activities and sport take appropriate steps to prepare for vigorous activity through an effective warm-up. A cool-down afterwards is equally important for injury prevention. This applies to all physical activities at all levels, including if you are a beginner. The specific benefits of the warm-up and cool-down are described above.

Dangerous training practices

There are many different exercise and training methods, some of which have been dealt with earlier in this book. However, some unconventional and unrecognised methods may also prove dangerous and cause injury or illness. Certain types of training are only suited to the very best performers, whose bodies require and are able to take the extra stresses and strains for top competition. If a novice performer attempts advanced training methods without working up towards them, injury is much more likely.

PRACTICAL APPLICATIONS

DANGEROUS TRAINING PRACTICES

Serious injuries and even deaths have been known to occur in javelin training. In long-distance running there have been athletes who have not prepared properly and who have suffered from severe heat exhaustion. Even very simple activities such as shooting at goal in hockey can be dangerous if players do not wait for safe moments to shoot. In gymnastics, horrendous spinal injuries have been caused by pushing young gymnasts too far and getting them to attempt moves that they are not ready for. Lasting back damage has been sustained in yoga classes that are inappropriate and do not take into account individual differences.

Whatever the method of training, it is vital that certain safety issues are addressed. Health and safety is very important whatever level you are at in your physical activities and sport.

Inadequate or inappropriate diet

As we have already seen, it is very important that a physical activities and sports performer eats and drinks appropriately. This includes a balanced diet and adequate intake of water before, during and after exercise.

 PRACTICAL APPLICATIONS

DEHYDRATION
Studies show that individuals who are dehydrated become ill. The body's systems become inefficient and the body cannot provide adequate blood flow to the skin, which reduces its ability to get rid of unwanted heat. If excess heat remains in the body, heat exhaustion is more likely. Fluid intake during prolonged exercise will make dehydration less likely and will slow the rise in body temperature.

Influence of alcohol or drugs

There are proven links between drug abuse or excessive alcohol consumption and illness. Those involved in physical activities either as a participant, a leader or an official should drink moderately (if at all) and avoid recreational or performance-enhancing drugs.

In recent years there has been an increase in sports people testing positive for drugs. This may either indicate an increase in drug use or suggest that the drug testers are getting better at their job! Many drugs that are taken to try to improve performance in sport have side effects, which may seriously damage the health of the athlete.

Fig 6.2.1 Water is the most important drink taken before, during and after exercise

PRACTICAL APPLICATIONS

ANABOLIC STEROIDS
These are man-made drugs that increase muscle growth if taken with vigorous training. They also enable the athlete to recover faster and therefore train even harder. The main problems with taking such drugs are:
- liver and kidneys can develop tumours
- the liver ceases to act properly, causing major health problems
- high blood pressure
- severe acne or spots
- shrinking of the testicles, reduced sperm count and the development of breasts in males
- growth of facial hair, baldness and deepening of the voice in females
- increase in aggression and other psychological problems.

Dangerous environment

The playing field, court or track can all have potential hazards associated with them. Local recreational pitches may have litter that is dangerous to physical activity and sports participants. Large stones, broken glass and even discarded hypodermic syringe needles can cause serious injury. In exercise classes in multiple-use facilities such as a church hall, there may be chairs stacked around the outside that may fall and potentially cause injury.

Weather conditions

The weather can cause problems for participants, leaders and officials alike. For example, if there is a thunderstorm there is a risk of being struck by lightning, especially in water-based activities. Severe hot weather can cause **dehydration** and heat exhaustion and severe cold weather can cause hypothermia.

Inappropriate or dangerous clothing

When you participate in physical activity and sport, at any level – from a 'kick around' in the park to preparing for an Olympic final – you must wear the correct clothing. Certain items of clothing can be dangerous – for example, training shoes are unsafe if not properly laced, and jewellery such as rings, necklaces and earrings can cause injury to the person wearing them or to other people. Clothing should also be appropriate to the weather conditions: lighter clothing for hot weather, warmer clothing in cold conditions.

Lifting and carrying equipment

Back strains and even broken limbs have been caused by incorrect methods of lifting and carrying sports equipment. The correct technique for lifting heavy equipment involves bending the knees rather than the back. Some equipment needs to be lifted with mechanical assistance, and if there are special instructions concerning the method of lifting or moving a particular piece of equipment these should always be followed.

Additional hazards can arise during assembly of equipment; for instance, a trampoline should only be put up by people who have been trained to do it properly, otherwise there is a danger of the trampoline's legs springing up and causing injury.

Inappropriate or damaged equipment

The equipment that is used in physical activity and sport should also be correct for the activity and the age/ability of the people involved. For example, in gymnastics the vaulting box should be at an appropriate height. For very young tennis players the rackets may be lighter and smaller than full size. Unsuitable equipment can cause injury; for example if a vault is too high there is a greater chance of the gymnast colliding with the box. A tennis player who has too heavy a racket may experience muscle strains in the arm.

Make sure that all equipment is 'fit for purpose': in other words, that it is in good working order and is safe to use. Damaged equipment can cause injury; for example, if a basketball backboard is damaged it may become loose and fall upon a competitor, causing serious injury.

Behaviour of other participants

Correct behaviour in physical activity and sport is important to injury prevention. If a child throws a discus out of turn it may well hit another child, causing a nasty injury. If a team player becomes overly aggressive and hits out at an opponent then, again, injury will occur. If a participant in canoeing decides to tip someone else out of their canoe then there is a risk of serious injury or even drowning.

Codes of behaviour are established so that all participants know what is expected of them when playing a particular sport or engaging in exercise and physical activities, and for safety reasons it is important to adhere to these codes.

Fig 6.2.2 Codes of behaviour are important

REDUCING RISKS AND PREVENTING INJURIES

The following are ways of helping to prevent the injuries or health problems identified above.

1 Make sure that you are fit for physical activity and sport. If you are to play an activity requiring stamina, make sure that you have good cardio-respiratory fitness. If, for example, in basketball, you are required to stretch suddenly make sure that you have worked on your flexibility to prevent injury. Be aware of the main principles of fitness training that have been covered in this book. Any exercise and training programme must take into account the individual. The participant's age, time available, equipment available and skill level must all be taken into consideration before the principles of training are applied.

2 Each participant must get to a particular skill level and have good skill technique before performing seriously in physical activity and sport. Exercise and training should include basic skills, which when practised enough become almost second nature. Injury is much less likely the higher your personal skill level. Ensure that skills and techniques follow technical models of how the skill ought to be performed to ensure personal health and safety.

3 Whatever the level of the physical activity or sport – whether it is serious competition or just recreational play – you should be prepared for it by carrying out an effective warm-up. This often includes some light activity to raise the body's temperature and to ensure better flexibility in muscles and ligaments. In team games the activity may include light jogging followed by a series of stretching exercises to prepare the muscles for sudden and prolonged movement. A cool-down is equally important and should take place immediately after exercise. The cool-down normally involves similar exercises to the warm-up – steady jogging and stretching. This enables any lactic acid to be dispersed and prevents muscle soreness during the days following the activity.

4 Always ensure that your training is safe. After warming up sufficiently your exercise regime should suit your age, ability and physical fitness. You should also ensure that you do not push yourself too hard and that you 'listen' to your body and stop if any exercise hurts or you are getting unduly fatigued.

5 The level of competition needs to match your ability level to prevent unnecessary injury. For example, boxers must box within their own weight category.

 PRACTICAL APPLICATIONS

EXERCISING SAFELY

Identify the individual's training goal.
Identify medium- and long-term goals.
Identify the fitness components to be improved.
Establish the energy systems to be used.
Identify the muscle groups that will be used.

Evaluate the fitness components involved.
Use a training diary.
Vary the programme to maintain motivation.
Include rest in the programme for recovery.
Evaluate and reassess goals.

Injury Statistics (Health and Safety Executive)

(The report covers a recent five-year period)

There were four fatal injuries in the sports and recreation industry: one death involved being struck by a vehicle; another resulted from an explosion; and one resulted from coming into contact with moving machinery.

Fatal injuries to members of the public:

- 'A child was crushed by an unsecured mobile goal post while playing on a football field. Children moved the posts from their usual secured storage place so that they could use them. The goal posts were very heavy and unstable, and needed secure fixing before use.'
- 'A man died when his jet ski collided with a similar water craft piloted by a friend. The jet skis had been inspected and serviced by the proprietor of the Jet Ski centre. Observers said the two men were not observing sufficient caution while piloting the craft. The coroner reported a verdict of accidental death. No blame was attached to the proprietors. An engineer found the craft to be in perfect working order.'
- 'A member of the public was killed when he crashed at a motor racing circuit. The man had been taking part in a motorcycle "experience" activity. The rider died as a result of head injuries sustained in the accident. The investigation revealed that there was no obvious cause of the accident.'

Of the 999 major injuries:

- 349 (35%) injuries resulted from a slip or trip (106 involved slipping on a slippery surface
- 75 involved lost footing, 62 involved falling over an obstruction and 60 involved slipping whilst playing sports)
- 227 (23%) injuries resulted from fall from a height (97 involved a fall from an animal, 30 involved a fall down stairs and 25 resulted from a fall from another object)
- 95 (10%) injuries resulted from being struck by a moving or falling object (17 involved being struck by an object falling from a shelf, table or stack, 15 were

struck by a door or ramp, 11 involved being struck by a falling piece of structure and 11 involved being struck by flying chips or nails)

- 79 (8%) injuries resulted from handling, lifting or carrying a load (of which 39 involved an awkward or sharp object and 24 involved a heavy object)
- 68 (7%) injuries resulted from being injured by an animal.

Non-fatal injuries to members of the public:

- In a five-year period there were 3,675 non-fatal injuries to members of the public in the sports and recreation industry. Of these 3,675 non-fatal injuries:
- 1,430 (39%) injuries resulted from a slip or trip (762 involved slipping whilst playing sports, 228 involved slipping on a slippery surface, 148 involved lost footing and 122 involved falling over an obstruction)
- 1,347 (37%) injuries resulted from a fall from a height (640 involved falling from an animal, 297 involved falling whilst playing sport and 126 involved a fall from a motor vehicle)
- 319 (9%) injuries resulted from striking a fixed object (216 involved walking into a fixed object, e.g. a wall, 43 involved walking into or striking another person and 21 stepped on a nail or other similar object).

COMMON TYPES OF SPORTS INJURIES

Head injuries

A likely head injury in sport is to be knocked unconscious and to suffer from concussion. Concussion is possible in contact sport, but is most common in boxing, skiing, rugby and football. It is caused by a hard blow to the head or by the head striking an object. When there is a violent blow to the head the brain bounces against the rigid bone of the skull. The brain's stabilising connective tissue and blood vessels may tear and this stops the normal passage of messages in the brain. The result is a feeling of headache, nausea, dizziness, increase in pupil size, sickness and confusion. If the player has suffered light concussion then they can return to play after about 15 minutes of rest following a medical check. If unconscious then check the airway is clear and call a trained first aider. A hospital visit is advisable. There may at least a week for a full recovery to be made after severe concussion. Post concussion syndrome can occur after weeks or months if proper treatment is not given after the injury.

> Injuries and their treatment are not directly examined in the specification but background knowledge of injuries will help your understanding of how to reduce risks and injuries.

PRACTICAL APPLICATIONS

CONCUSSION
Professional rugby players are not allowed to play for three weeks after experiencing concussion.

Wales's rugby player Alix Popham nursed a sore head after being knocked unconscious during his team's match against South Africa in 2004. The No. 8 had to be stretchered off the pitch and spent the night in hospital. Luckily, Popham escaped serious injury thanks to the quick thinking of teammate Ceri Sweeney, who stopped him swallowing his tongue. Head injuries can occur in all sports and must be treated seriously.

Spinal injury

Any injury to the spine should be treated extremely seriously. It could result in lasting damage to someone's health and their fitness to operate normally let alone to play sport. Damage to the spinal cord may cause very painful conditions. A break in the cord high up in the spine is usually fatal.

If there is a suspected injury to the spine it is important to get expert help immediately without moving the injured person. Moving a person who has a spinal injury could make matters much worse.

PRACTICAL APPLICATIONS

Spinal injuries can be caused by incidents such as a collapsed rugby scrum or falling off a horse in equine events.

Fractures

Bone fractures can be serious injuries. As well as damaging the bone they often injure the tissues around the bone such as tendons, ligaments, muscles and skin. A fracture occurs when there is a physical impact to the arm, leg or bone or an indirect blow. Anyone involved in contact sports is in danger of sustaining a fractured bone.

A fracture causes swelling and progressive bruising and a lot of pain during movement. You may also be able to see that the limb with the suspected fracture looks awkward and that the bone isn't in the right place.

To treat the fracture, cover and elevate the injured limb and keep it completely still. The casualty should go to hospital for treatment. The limb will probably be put in a cast to keep it completely still while the bone heals. Casts have traditionally been made of plaster, which can be quite heavy, but nowadays doctors are increasingly using lightweight plastic casts. The injured person can be back in training after 5–12 weeks.

Dislocations

Dislocation involves movement of a joint from its normal position and is caused by a blow or a fall. When a joint has a lot of pressure put upon it in a certain direction, the bones that usually join in the joint disconnect. The joint capsule often tears because of this movement of bones, along with the ligaments involved. A dislocated joint looks out of place and misshapen. The exerciser or sports person will have limited movement and will experience severe pain.

Soft tissue injuries

These are injuries that affect muscles, tendons, ligaments and skin.

Sprain

This is a tear to a ligament and is often caused by an overstretch. Ankles, knees and wrists are very susceptible to sprains.

PRACTICAL APPLICATIONS

ANKLE SPRAIN

Ankle sprains are common among people involved in sport or outdoor activities. Going over on your ankle causes this injury. Sometimes a 'snap' or 'tear' is felt or heard.
There are three grades of severity:
- Grade 1: pain turning foot in or out
- Grade 2: swelling
- Grade 3: huge swelling and difficulty walking

Treatment of an ankle sprain involves rest, ice, compression and elevation. Do not remove the shoe until ice has reduced the ankle swelling.

Recovery takes between one week and three months depending on the grade of injury. The usual recovery time is two weeks.

Strain

This is a twist or tear to a muscle or a tendon. Causes include overuse of the joint, force or overstretching. There are three degrees of strain:

1 First degree – this is when only a few muscle fibres are torn and there is mild swelling. There is only a little pain.
2 Second degree – this is when there is a little more tearing of the muscle fibres. There is much more pain, along with swelling and stiffness.
3 Third degree – this is when there is a total rupture or tear in the muscle. There is a considerable amount of pain and severe swelling.

Blisters

A blister is the body's way of trying to put protection between the skin and what is causing friction – e.g. in a footballer's case, their boot.

The skin is in various layers. Friction and force cause these layers to tear. Fluid called serum flows in between the damaged skin layers, producing a bubble of liquid. The pain comes about when this swelling rubs against another surface.

Blisters can be a real nuisance to sports performers, especially in team games.

 PRACTICAL APPLICATIONS

BLISTERS IN PORTUGAL EURO 04
Blisters forced David Beckham, Sol Campbell and Steven Gerrard to miss training ahead of England's Euro 2004 game against Switzerland.

This could have been due to the very hot weather, since heat causes the foot to swell. This can be made worse if the players have been wearing sandals or walking around bare-footed. If this is the case, then their boots may not fit comfortably.

Footballers put their feet through an enormous amount of stress. For example, when they go up for a header, the body's entire weight is coming down again on a small area, placing it under a huge amount of pressure.

To treat blisters, the first thing you have to do is cleanse the skin with a sterilising solution. Then, with a sterilised needle, puncture the blister. Having done that, make sure you do not damage the skin; otherwise it could create further problems. The next step is to put a protective covering over the blister to prevent infections. Chiropodists use something called hydro gel to cover the blister. It is like a second skin and protects the foot from further damage.

The amount of time a blister takes to heal depends upon how big it is, but on average a couple of days is enough.

Blood blisters are a mix of blood and serum. Some can get as big as three or four inches in width and length. The most important thing to remember is to put a protective barrier around a blood blister until it heals.

You can prevent blisters by wearing in your football boots (or other sports footwear) properly to soften up the leather. Wear them around the house as this will help to mould the boot around your foot's shape.

ALTERNATIVE TREATMENTS

The medical profession is increasingly aware and more accepting of alternative treatments for injured sportspeople. There is no reason why some treatments should not be tried as long as the practitioner is appropriately qualified. Personal recommendation is best. If you hear of someone who has benefited from alternative treatment, find out details about the therapist.

Acupuncture

Acupuncture is a traditional form of Chinese medicine, which has been in existence for over 3,000 years. It involves inserting needles into the skin in strategic places called acupuncture points situated along energy channels called meridians. The Chinese believe that energy flows around the body in these channels. If it flows freely, the body is in a healthy state, but if there is a problem, energy stagnates and pain and other symptoms may develop. The stimulation of these acupuncture points frees this stagnation and allows the body to return to a healthy state. Some GPs are now trained in acupuncture or will refer you to a well-qualified acupuncturist.

Homeopathy

Homeopathy is the treatment of 'like with like'. Minute doses of substances that can cause signs of illness in a healthy person are used to treat the same symptoms in a sick person. Tiny doses of plant, animal or mineral materials are soaked in alcohol and then diluted and shaken vigorously. The more a substance is diluted, the stronger its therapeutic or helpful effect. Testing the substance on healthy volunteers and noting the symptoms produced have determined the effect of each remedy.

RISK ASSESSMENT

To be able to prepare a risk assessment it is important to identify:

- **the health and safety hazards in a given situation**. This includes identifying equipment faults, use of chemicals and other substances hazardous to health and the possibility of spillages.
- **the purpose of the assessment**. Identify the level of risk. The assessment is designed mostly to minimise injury to participants and workers. It is also designed to ensure that the activity involved can be successful, with no injury or accident but hopefully keeping the pleasure and excitement. A safe environment is crucial if physical activity is to be successful.
- **the risks that are involved.** Participants, coaches, supervisors, etc. must be aware of their responsibilities in limiting the risks in any sports activity. The risks should be calculated, specialist equipment used and record sheets and other documents kept up to date.
- **procedures for monitoring or checking that risks are kept to a minimum.** If there are any changes to the planning of an activity, these should be reviewed to identify their levels of success. There may be other equipment one may buy to make the environment safe or new procedures to be used. All this must be planned within an identified time cycle.

Identifying hazards

The area in which the activity takes place must be looked at carefully to recognise hazards that may be present. The facilities and equipment that are used in physical activities often carry warnings of possible injuries and these must be noted.

> **Risk assessment**
> Risk assessment is the technique by which you measure the chances of an accident happening, anticipate what the consequences would be and plan actions to prevent it.

> **Be able to** identify a hazard for each area named in the specification:
> - gymnasium/sports hall/fitness centre
> - playing field
> - artificial outdoor areas
> - court areas
> - outdoor adventurous areas.

⚽ PRACTICAL APPLICATIONS

An astro-turf, all-weather surface can cause friction burns if a player falls or slides on to the surface.

There may be obvious risks associated with the activity, the equipment or the facilities provided – for example, in a swimming pool or in an athletics session involving throwing.

The main causes of accidents are:

- objects falling – e.g. a container falling off a shelf in a leisure centre
- trips and falls – e.g. a path leading up to a sports facility may be uneven
- electric shock – e.g. from a hi-fi used to provide music for an aerobics session.
- crowds – e.g. being jostled or crushed by supporters at a football match
- poisoning – e.g. by toxic chemicals used in a swimming pool
- being hit by something – e.g. a javelin
- fire – e.g. in the changing rooms of a sports centre
- explosion – e.g. in the store area of a leisure centre
- asphyxiation – e.g. by chemicals used for cleaning

Identify who might be harmed

Care must be taken of those who may not be fully aware of risks, for instance children or those with learning difficulties, or someone new to a job in a leisure centre or a beginner in a sports activity. Once those who are at particular risk have been identified, an assessment of how they might be harmed needs to be made and safety procedures put into place to protect them.

Evaluate whether existing safety measures are adequate

There must be an assessment of how dangerous a particular hazard is and then whether the risks associated with that hazard are high, moderate or low. If the hazard is particularly dangerous and the risks are high, more care clearly needs to be taken.

In many cases it may be possible to remove the hazard altogether, for instance an uneven path is put out of bounds or a broken indoor football goal removed from a sports hall.

In some cases the hazard has to be made safer to reduce the risks. For example glass in a door that is used frequently used can be replaced by non-breakable plastic, or a trampoline can be surrounded by additional safety mats.

The risks arising from some hazards can be limited by using protective equipment, as when people wear protective gloves when handling cleaning equipment or a rugby player wears a gum-shield.

Hazard
Something that has the potential to cause harm.

Risk
The chance that someone will be harmed by the hazard.

Don't get the terms 'hazard' and 'injury' mixed up. If you are asked to identify a hazard do not give the injury that might be caused by the hazard. For instance, a hazard might be a broken bottle on a playing field – the hazard is not the cut that might be caused by the broken glass.

PRACTICAL APPLICATIONS

An example of a piece of protective equipment in a physical activity is a squash player wearing protective goggles to minimise the risk of impact with the ball.

The hazard is often supervised so that the risks are minimised. A supervisory function is performed by, for example, a lifeguard at a swimming pool, spotters around a trampoline or a coach supporting a gymnast on the beam.

Fig 6.2.3 The risks arising from some hazards can be limited by using protective equipment

THE IMPORTANCE OF PERSONAL HYGIENE

Good personal hygiene should be an important consideration for all participants, coaches, leaders and officials in physical activity. Hygienic habits will minimise the spreading of infections among team-mates or fellow club members, for example.

Hair

This should be washed regularly and in many physical activities should be tied back to avoid accidents. If there is any indication that you may have nits then you must seek treatment straight away. Remember that having nits is not an indication of dirty hair – it is just an indication that you have been near someone else with nits.

Nails

These should be kept thoroughly clean and preferably short because long nails can harbour many germs. Each time you wash it is a good idea to pay particular attention to cleaning your nails. In many physical activities it may be appropriate to have short nails because of the risk of scratching or injuring another participant.

Skin

You should wash or shower after physical activity because of the build-up of sweat, which may harbour bacteria and, of course, will also give off an unpleasant odour. Washing your hands regularly will help to prevent infection and in particular you should wash your hands thoroughly after going to the toilet.

✓ Athlete's foot
This is a fungal infection of the feet. It causes intense itchiness and can also get very sore. You should seek treatment if you think you have athlete's foot. Wash and dry your feet thoroughly and avoid being barefoot in communal changing rooms because the infection is easily passed on to others.

Feet

Again it is very important to keep these clean and to change your socks regularly, particularly after physical exercise. Wash your feet thoroughly and also dry them well because feet that are left damp can attract infections such as athlete's foot.

Clothing

Again in the interests of avoiding infection, clothes should be changed regularly and washed and thoroughly dried. A daily change of underclothes is recommended, as is a complete change of clothes after physical activity.

When engaging in exercise and sport, wear clothing that is designed to be appropriate and comfortable. It should also be well fitting to prevent blisters, chafeing and discomfort.

 ACTIVITY 4

TASK
Make a poster about personal hygiene to be displayed in changing rooms. Include information that is practical and clear.

CHALLENGE
Design a leaflet that could be given to all pupils who represent the school in physical activities. The leaflet should give hygiene tips and problems that could occur if hygiene standards are not maintained.

? REVIEW QUESTIONS

1 What are the main training principles?
2 Describe the training principles.
3 How would you apply these principles to plan a targeted range of exercise or a training programme?
4 What is meant by the FITT principle?
5 What is meant by a hazard in physical activities?
6 What hazards are associated with the gymnasium/sports hall/fitness centre?
7 What hazards are associated with a playing field and an artificial outdoor area?
8 What hazards are there associated with court areas?
9 What hazards are associated with outdoor adventurous areas?
10 How would you reduce the risk of hazards in each of these areas?
11 Why is personal hygiene important in physical activities?

E EXAM-STYLE QUESTIONS

Multiple choice
1 Which of the following statements does NOT follow the FITT principle?
  a You should take vigorous exercise at least three times per week.
  b Each exercise session should be at least 20 minutes long.
  c The exercise programme should include different types of activities.
  d You must eat at least five portions of fruit and vegetables each day.
2 Why is personal hygiene important in physical education?
  a to avoid minor infections
  b to be a more successful performer
  c to be able to lift and carry equipment safely
  d none of the above.

3 Which of the following is a potential hazard of a school playing field?
   a correct footwear
   b discarded litter
   c the sports equipment
   d other players.

Short answer questions

1 There are recognised principles of training. One of these is reversibility.
   What is meant by reversibility when training for an active lifestyle?   **(2 marks)**
2 Outline a six-week training programme showing how you would
   apply the principles of specificity and overload.   **(6 marks)**
3 Describe an occasion when correct carrying technique will reduce
   the chance of injury during or preparing for a physical activity.   **(2 marks)**
4 Describe three ways of minimising risks when following an active
   lifestyle.   **(3 marks)**
5 Identify a hazard in an outdoor adventurous activity and explain
   how you would reduce the risks associated with that hazard.   **(4 marks)**

 WHAT YOU NEED TO KNOW

• the short-term and long-term effects of an active lifestyle

• application of training principles to plan a targeted range of exercise or training programme

• the FITT principle for exercise and training

• the potential hazards related to physical activities

• how to reduce the risks and injuries posed by hazards

• the importance of personal hygiene.

SECTION

2

OPPORTUNITIES AND PATHWAYS FOR INVOLVEMENT IN PHYSICAL ACTIVITIES

LEVELS OF PARTICIPATION IN SPORT AND PHYSICAL ACTIVITY

LEARNING GOALS

By the end of this chapter you should be able to:

- describe the levels of participation in physical activity in the UK (SC)
- describe the effects of the media on following an active, healthy lifestyle
- describe the effects of sponsorship and funding on following an active, healthy lifestyle

PATTERNS OF PARTICIPATION IN SPORT AND PHYSICAL ACTIVITY IN THE UK

Sport
Competition between individuals or teams that is organised and includes physical activity.

It is important to recognise what we mean by the term sport.

Sport involves a competitive activity. Competition can be among individuals (for example, in skiing or the high jump) or between teams (for example, in hockey or football). Sport often involves people watching – i.e. spectators. Spectators often pay to watch if professional sport is involved; for example, those who wish to watch county cricket have to pay to enter the ground.

Sports also involve rules so that there is no unfair advantage to a team or an individual and no cheating. In sport there is also usually a defined place to play, for example, a netball court or a football pitch. These sports places usually have boundaries — for example, the sideline on a hockey pitch. Sport also involves a certain amount of luck or chance; for example, the ball in tennis may hit the net cord and travel over to the other side rather than your side, thus winning a point.

We use lots of different terms when describing sports and related activities. The following terminology is sometimes used to categorise different types of sport:

- invasion games
- target games
- court games
- field sports.

Invasion games

The object of this type of game is to invade the opponent's territory, as if you are at war with the opposition – which of course you are not! Rugby, netball and football are examples of invasion games.

Target games

As the name suggests, the aim of these games is to hit certain targets. They involve accuracy of judgement, often called 'marksmanship'. Target games include golf and archery.

Court games

These games include tennis, squash and volleyball. There is usually no contact between the players because they are kept apart by a net, although in squash both players occupy the same space.

Field sports

These are often, but not always, associated with rural areas. Sports such as hunting, shooting and fishing are field sports and are linked with killing animals for food, although the point of most field sports is the competition between man and the animal he or she wishes to kill. Many people who participate in field sports describe the 'thrill of the chase' or the 'thrill of the catch' as the most enjoyable aspect. Others oppose these activities on the grounds that they are cruel and unsporting, involving an unfair human advantage over animals that have no choice about participating and often experience a great deal of stress and suffering before being killed.

Amateurs and professionals

Sport can be played as an amateur or as a professional. An example of an amateur player would be a netball player who plays for her local club or a rugby player who plays for his local club. Neither of these players would receive any money for playing the sport. An example of a professional would be a county cricket player or a football player who plays in the Nationwide League. Both of these players play for a living – it is their job to play the sport and therefore they are called professional players. There are some players who are called semi-professionals who receive money for playing but do not earn enough to make a living from the sport and therefore have other jobs to support them.

Leisure

This is a wide term covering the many different activities we are involved in that have nothing to do with work or school. Leisure activities are things we choose to do rather than have to do. They may involve sport, but not necessarily: watching TV, going to the cinema and reading a book are all leisure activities, as are skateboarding in the park or going for a bike ride with friends. For many of us, particularly with the spread of labour-saving machines, the time available for leisure has increased over the last 100 years.

People participate in leisure activities for a number of reasons – for instance, to escape the stresses of everyday life and do something enjoyable, or to meet other people and make friends.

Recreation

Recreation is a term for an active aspect of leisure. Recreation is not curling up in front of the TV but doing something useful and constructive, whether a sports activity or something like cooking or gardening. People's ideas of what counts as recreation differ: some people would view cooking or gardening as anything but recreation! Recreation involves a state of mind – viewing the activity as not doing work but active enjoyment that helps us to relax and escape stress.

✓ **Leisure**
'Time in which there is an opportunity for choice.'
'An activity, apart from the obligations of work, family and society, to which the individual turns at will, for either relaxation, diversion, or broadening experiences and his spontaneous social participation, the free exercise of his creative capacities.'

Recreation
An enjoyable activity that refreshes you and gives you more energy.

PRACTICAL APPLICATIONS

Outdoor and adventurous recreation activities involve individual challenge, for example climbing and canoeing. Many of these activities are in the natural environment. There has been an increase in interest in outdoor and adventurous sports with the term 'extreme sports' also being used to describe sports that have elements of danger associated with them. Mountain biking, climbing, windsurfing and skateboarding are very popular now.

Fig 7.1 Some extreme sports are very popular

Lifetime sports

These are sports such as badminton and golf that can be carried on throughout our lives. Increasing age is not an insuperable obstacle to participation in sport. Providing you choose suitable activities, you can stay fit and active as well as being socially involved with other people.

The leisure industry

This has grown rapidly over the last 20 years, as people have acquired more leisure time and become willing to spend money on leisure activities. The sale of leisure goods, services and access to facilities is now a profitable industry. Sport is also very commercialised, with events and competitors being sponsored for (and paid) large sums of money.

Participation rates
This refers to the number of people within a group who are involved in sport compared with those who are not. For example, in a school the participation rate of girls in extra-curricular sport could be 30 per cent. In other words, 3 out of every 10 girls in the school are regular members of a sports team or club.

 PRACTICAL APPLICATIONS

The leisure industry comprises the products and services that surround leisure activities. The products for leisure include trainers and other sports clothing, equipment and DVDs. Leisure services include cinemas, sports stadia, skateboard parks and leisure centres. Large multi-national companies such as MGM often control the business of leisure.

Leisure centres and health clubs

In recent years there has been a tremendous growth in the number of health clubs and leisure centres in both the private sector (owned by a commercial company) and the public sector (run by local councils and subsidised by the taxpayer). Private clubs saw massive growth from 2002 to 2007, for example Livingwell, LA Fitness, Fitness First and the David Lloyd Centres. There was also demand for private trainers, i.e. fitness professionals who work with individuals for an hourly fee. Other services benefited from this health and fitness boom, such as nutrition advice and beauty treatment. With the economic downturn in 2008 and 2009, the leisure industry may well experience a fall in profits as consumers cut their personal costs.

The specification states that you should know the participation trends and be able to explain some of the reasons for participation or non-participation. This includes:

Understanding and application of patterns and trends of participation in different age groups.

Numbers of people participating regularly in sporting activity at the recommended level (using established and reliable sources such as UK Sport).

Reasons for participation and non-participation in physical activities and following an active, healthy lifestyle.

www.statistics.gov.uk
Full of statistical information about participation in physical activities by different groups of people.

www.uksport.gov.uk
Has recent research which shows that participation rates are declining in many physical activities.

PRACTICAL APPLICATIONS

THE BENEFITS OF SPORT – SOME FACTS
Sport is getting youngsters away from crime and helping fight drug abuse, according to reports commissioned by Sport England. In Bristol there has been a 40 per cent reduction in crime levels on the Southmead Estate since the first sport development worker was appointed.

There are many examples of inequality in sport. Groups of people who are not getting a fair chance in sport include (but are not limited to):

- minority ethnic groups
- people with disabilities
- women.
- the 50+ age group.

Participation in sports, games and physical activities

In a variety of studies it has been shown that about three quarters of adults had taken part in some sport, game or physical activity during the last twelve months.

In terms of participation the five most popular sports, games or physical activities among adults in the UK are (figures are approximate):

- walking (46 per cent)
- swimming (35 per cent)
- keep fit/yoga – including aerobics and dance exercise (22 per cent)
- cycling (19 per cent)
- cue sports – billiards, snooker and pool (17 per cent).

Source: Household Survey (2002)

Participation rates by sex and age

A difference persists in the participation levels of men and women, with far more men getting involved either as sports players or spectators: about 51 per cent of men compared with 36 per cent of women. Forty-four per cent of men and 31 per cent of women who participate in at least one activity (excluding walking and darts) belong to a club. Overall, men are more likely than women to participate in an organised competition, with about 40 per cent of men competing compared with 14 per cent of women. It is still thought by some people that being good at or interested in sport is unfeminine, thus reinforcing male dominance in sport and sport coverage.

PRACTICAL APPLICATIONS

In tennis there is a huge discrepancy between men's and women's prize money, with women getting far less. The media show lot of interest in women tennis players but this is often because of their looks rather than their performance.

Fig 7.2 The media often focus on the looks of female tennis players

On the positive side, more women are now involved in physical exercise and interested in health and fitness. Participation rates for women in previously all-male sports such as football and rugby are now much higher and continue to grow.

The proportion of adults who take part in at least one sport or physical activity generally decreases with age. Seventy-seven per cent of 16- to 19-year-olds take part in at least one physical activity (including walking) compared with 30 per cent of people aged 70 and over. Participation rates, which excluded walking, range from 72 per cent of 16- to 19-year-olds to 14 per cent of people aged 70 and over.

Walking is the most popular activity for all age groups. Participation rates in walking increase from 29 per cent of those aged 16 to 19 to 40 per cent of those aged 45 to 59, after which they decline.

Participation in some activities is very strongly related to age. For example, activities such as soccer, cue sports, running and cycling are generally more popular with the younger age groups and the rates of participation for these activities decrease with age. However, participation in golf is maintained at a fairly similar level up to age 69, with the average age of participants about 42. Participation rates in swimming and keep fit/yoga remain at similar levels between the ages of 16 and 44, after which they fall. Participants in bowls peak among 60- to 69-year-olds.

 PRACTICAL APPLICATIONS

The London Marathon is an event that combines seriously competitive runners, those who are looking for a personal challenge and those who are running to make money for charity.

About 35,000 runners participated in the London Marathon in April 2008. Elite athletes, six Masai warriors, a 101-year-old man and amateurs hoping to raise thousands of pounds for charity were among those taking part.

Kenya's Martin Lel set a new course record at the London Marathon as he defended his title to win the race for the third time in four years. Lel finished in a time of 2 hours 5 minutes and 15 seconds.

In sport, as in life, individuals and particular groups may feel discriminated against in terms of access to sport.

UK Sport has a written statement regarding equity in sport: 'Equity is about recognising and removing the barriers faced by people involved, or wanting to be involved, in sport. It is about changing the culture of sport to one that values

✓ **Sports equity**
This is concerned with fairness in sport and equality of access. It is about recognising inequalities and taking steps to address them. The aim is to make sport equally accessible to all members of society, whatever their age, ability, gender, race, ethnicity, sexuality or social/economic status.

 PRACTICAL APPLICATIONS

UK Sport, formerly called the Sports Council, produced a report called 'Better Quality Sport for All'. This report highlighted the need to enable people to learn basic sports skills that could be built upon to achieve sporting excellence.

The report highlighted strategies designed to help people:
- develop the skills and competence to enjoy sport
- follow a lifestyle which includes active participation in sport and recreation

- achieve their personal goals at whatever their chosen level of involvement in sport
- developing excellence and achieve success in sport at the highest level.

The report stated that everyone has the right to play sport. Whether it is for fun, for health, to enjoy the natural environment or to win, everyone should have the opportunity to enjoy sport. The challenge was to make England 'the sporting nation'.

diversity and enables the full involvement of disadvantaged groups in every aspect of sport.'

THE EFFECTS OF THE MEDIA ON FOLLOWING AN ACTIVE, HEALTHY LIFESTYLE

Television companies spend an enormous amount of money on the broadcasting rights to sports-related events. To view certain events such as boxing, the subscriber often has to make an extra payment (pay-per-view). Sky, for example, holds the rights to many Premiership football games, which can only be viewed if you subscribe to a Sky package. Digital TV has also influenced sport — and not always to anyone's benefit.

The terrestrial channels such as BBC and ITV have lost many of the major sports events, which results in ludicrous situations such as the BBC news being unable to show a clip of a boxing match because the rights to that match are owned by another company. In short, there has never before been so much sport on TV but because of satellite TV dominating this coverage, only those who can afford to subscribe have access to many sports events.

Distribution of coverage among different types of sport is also uneven, with football getting by far the most. Male sport also still dominates, although there is a refreshing interest in women's football, for instance.

 PRACTICAL APPLICATIONS

TYPES OF MEDIA
- television: BBC – ITV – Channel 4 – Channel 5 – satellite – cable – digital – factual/fiction/advertising
- press: broadsheets – tabloids – local – national – daily – weekly – magazines – periodicals
- radio: national – local – public service – commercial
- cinema: feature films (USA/UK/Bollywood, etc.) – documentaries

The rules of sport have been influenced by the media. For instance, in hockey the obstruction rule was modified to make the sport more watchable. In cricket the third umpire in the form of a video replay analysis has come into force, largely due to the influence of TV. There has been a similar development in rugby football. The armchair spectator can now see the event at every angle and the officials' decisions are laid bare for scrutiny, hence the need for new technology to aid the decision-makers on the field of play.

Event programming has sometimes been revised to meet the needs of the TV companies. Football fans, for instance, are finding that their team may play on a Sunday at 6.00pm, not a traditional timeslot for the game. Olympic Games events are often scheduled at unsuitable times because TV companies are beaming them around the world, across different time zones.

The extent of media involvement has also influenced the amount of sponsorship and advertising revenue available to participants, clubs and other sports organisations. This has brought much-welcomed money into sport, but some may argue that this has only reached a small number of participants in a small number of sports and may well have led to reduced participation in minority sports and other physical activities.

From a more positive perspective, the media can help to increase participation in physical activity and sport as well as reinforce the need to follow a healthy, active lifestyle. You only have to see the increased activity on municipal tennis courts during the Wimbledon fortnight to appreciate that watching sport can stimulate participation.

Fig 7.3 Wimbledon fortnight can stimulate participation in tennis

Our interest in playing a sport is particularly increased when the media highlights the success of UK sports performers. There was a surge of interest in cycling and swimming, for instance, after success in the Beijing Olympics.

Promotional campaigns for physical activity and a healthy lifestyle

The media frequently represents physical activity in a positive light and there are often features on the news and current affairs programmes that relate to healthy lifestyles – for example, healthy eating, giving up smoking or reducing the consumption of alcohol.

The media can also be guilty of reinforcing unhealthy lifestyles through attractive characters in dramas and soaps who indulge in unhealthy habits such as smoking or excessive drinking.

Promotional campaigns for healthy behaviour form part of the media's role in public service broadcasting. They are used to educate the public about health issues such as alcohol, with the aim of influencing individuals to change their behaviour. They often cover several dimensions of an issue – in the case of alcohol, not only the health consequences of excessive drinking but the risks posed by drink driving. Good campaigns inform as well as warn, for example by

www.dh.gov.uk /en/Publichealth/ Healthimprovement/Health yliving/index.htm
Has information about promotional campaigns for improving health for all ages.

www.healthyschools.gov.uk/
Has details of the 'healthy schools initiative' with promotional examples.

providing information about responsible drinking, and standard unit sizes for the laws relating to alcohol. Promotion campaigns may be aimed at a general audience or a specific audience segment, such as youth.

The media also includes the Internet and there are a number of websites that promote healthy lifestyles. See the list on page 130.

ACTIVITY 1

TASK

Collect or record an example of a health promotion campaign from any aspect of the media. Summarise the message and assess how effective you think it would be in changing people's attitudes and lifestyles.

CHALLENGE

Write your own promotion leaflet for a healthy lifestyle – aim it for a year 7 audience. What messages are you trying to get across?

Anti-crime initiatives using sport

Widespread media coverage is devoted to young people and crime. The popular press have raised the profile of antisocial behaviour and the use of Antisocial Behaviour Orders (ASBOs) to tackle this problem. Other initiatives try to deal with the root cause of unacceptable behaviour. Some of these initiatives use sport and physical activity to encourage more acceptable behaviour and to combat boredom. It is thought that many people who commit crime in this country have been socially excluded – in other words, their lifestyle falls below the normal threshold in our society and their opportunities are more limited. Those who are dependent on drugs may turn to crime to 'feed' their habit. Unemployed people may lack the financial means to be involved in sports and other physical activities.

Physical activity has often been viewed as a way of helping to combat crime, particularly among children and young people. Sports development activity is based on this assumption. Anecdotal evidence suggests that involvement in physical activity and sport reduces criminal behaviour by providing a distraction or an alternative pastime; there is little evidence that it directly reduces causal criminal behaviour.

✓ Antisocial Behaviour Orders

ASBOs are designed to prevent behaviour including theft, intimidation, drunkenness and violence by individuals and families who make life difficult for their communities. The orders often include restrictions on entering a geographical area or shop but can include bans on specific acts, such as swearing in public. Juveniles – who are usually protected by law from being named – can be identified to ensure the community involved know the ASBO has been imposed.

PRACTICAL APPLICATIONS

DIFFERENT VIEWS ON ASBOS

View Number 1

I work with young people at a pupil referral unit, many of whom have ASBOs. It does very little to stop the young people carrying on as normal. More money should be spent on preventing the causes of antisocial behaviour such as poor parenting, education and a lack of facilities for things like sport.

View Number 2

I for one am happy that these ASBOs are actually being handed out. Britain is under siege by these young people who intimidate the local populace. It all stems back to poor parenthood. It is sad that it has got to the state where discipline has to be given by the law when it is the responsibility of the parent. People say the young people have nothing to do! Go to school, play a sport for a team, get a hobby. What a pitiful excuse to say that one has nothing to do and so decides to terrorise the neighbourhood!

EFFECTS OF SPONSORSHIP AND FUNDING ON THE ABILITY TO FOLLOW AN ACTIVE, HEALTHY LIFESTYLE

Physical activity and sports organisations have a number of different sources of funding.

Grants

Grants are usually made available to the public and voluntary sectors (more about these in Chapter 8 page 139). Funding is available for private-sector projects from local or national government or the European Union, providing the project benefits the local population. Buildings and equipment are typically funded by grants. Many grants involve the sports organisation putting forward a percentage of the funds themselves, for example, 50 per cent from the government and 50 per cent self-funded.

Subsidies

If local authorities or councils tried to cover all the costs of sport, few people would be able to participate, for example, in swimming. Instead there is a system of subsidies whereby members of public pay a certain cost and the local authority pays the rest. Taxpayers fund these subsidies via local government.

Membership fees

All sports organisations which have a membership – usually the voluntary sector – can take a significant proportion of their income from membership fees. For example, members of a hockey club may pay an annual membership fee plus a 'match fee' for each game they play.

The National Lottery

This is an important source of grants for sport, as well as funding for world-class performers. Sport England, Sport Scotland and Sport Wales are lottery funds and these support sport at all levels. UK Sport is also lottery funded and this in turn funds high-performance sport in the UK.

Sponsorship

The influence of sponsorship on the development of physical activity and sport has been enormous. The exercise and sport market is now big business, with large amounts of money being spent by commercial companies on sports participants and events. For example, a company such as Adidas might sponsor a top-class tennis player to wear a particular style of training shoe. At the other end of the scale, a local hockey club may attract a small amount of money from a local business to go towards the first team kit.

The increasingly fashionable status of sports clothing has also led to a significant increase in sponsorship. For instance, there has been a huge increase in sales of training shoes. Many people wear 'trainers' who would never dream of participating in sport! Commercial companies recognise that top sports stars can be fashion role models for the young and therefore use them in advertising campaigns.

On the other hand, sports sponsorship is increasingly difficult to find for the 'middle-ranking sports', according to independent research commissioned by the Sports Sponsorship Advisory Service. A report presented to national governing bodies blames the current climate on sports' inability to attract sufficient media coverage. Sports sponsorship can be a vital ingredient in the financing of governing bodies' activities. Many sports, however, are unable to attract sponsors because they cannot get television coverage. Sport must also begin to understand the value of its intellectual property rights and how best to market them in a rapidly changing marketplace.

The main points regarding sponsorship are:

- Sponsors continue to seek image enhancement and brand awareness through sponsorship and see this as largely dependent on broadcast and other media coverage.
- Sponsors are also looking to sell their products, develop promotional opportunities and demonstrate that they are good corporate citizens.
- Sponsors continue to be attracted to the 'top ten' sports and/or to community based activity; 'middle ranking' sports are rarely considered.
- Women's sport has the potential to attract more sponsors but to date most of that potential is unfulfilled.
- Many sports are becoming more commercially aware but some do not fully understand the implications of sponsorship and sponsors' demands.

 REVIEW QUESTIONS

1 What are the main participation rates for different age groups in the UK?
2 What is the percentage of people participating regularly in a sporting activity at the recommended level in the UK?
3 How do the media affect participation in an active, healthy lifestyle?
4 How does sponsorship and funding affect participation in an active, healthy lifestyle?

 EXAM-STYLE QUESTIONS

Multiple choice questions
1 Which of the following statements is the most accurate about participation rates in sports and physical activities in the UK?
  a The proportion of adults who take part in at least one sport or physical activity generally decreases with age.
  b The proportion of children who take part in sport or physical activity increases with age.
  c The proportion of old people who take part in sport or physical activity increases with age.
  d The proportion of women who do not participate in sport or physical activity decreases with age.
2 What is meant by physical activity participation rates?
  a number of people who attend PE lessons
  b number of people who watch sport
  c number of people who learn sports skills quickly
  d number of people who are involved in sport

Short answer questions

1 Explain how the media promotes an active healthy lifestyle.   **(6 marks)**
2 Why are there gender differences in participation in physical
   activity at ages 15–19?   **(4 marks)**
3 In what ways do the media promote an active lifestyle?   **(5 marks)**
4 Describe a media promotional campaign for an active, healthy
   lifestyle.   **(4 marks)**

WHAT YOU NEED TO KNOW

- the levels of participation in physical activities for different age groups

- the number for people participating regularly in sporting activity at the
  recommended level ⓢⓒ

- the effects of the media on following an active, healthy lifestyle

- the effects of sponsorship and funding on following an active, healthy
  lifestyle

CHAPTER 8

REASONS FOR PARTICIPATION AND NON-PARTICIPATION IN PHYSICAL ACTIVITIES

LEARNING GOALS

By the end of this chapter you should be able to:

- identify and explain the reasons for participation in physical activity
- identify and explain the reasons for non-participation in physical activity.
- describe the role of the local authority in promoting physical activities
- describe the role of private enterprise in promoting physical activities
- describe the role of voluntary organisations in promoting physical activities
- describe the role of national organisations in promoting physical activities
- describe the role of Olympic organisations in promoting physical activities.

REASONS FOR FOLLOWING AN ACTIVE, HEALTHY LIFESTYLE

Many factors influence whether people participate in or watch sport. Some people show no interest in sports whatsoever but are nevertheless interested in keeping healthy and try to do some exercise as well as being careful what they eat.

The reasons that many people get involved in sport include:

- benefits to health and fitness – sport can make us fitter and therefore healthier
- benefits to well-being – many people report that they feel better after participating in sport. Certain hormones are released during exercise which can help us to feel more optimistic about life and better about ourselves
- relief from stress – people often use sport as an escape from the pressure of working life. By playing sport we can release some of our pent-up frustrations and aggressions – for example, by hitting a squash ball really hard
- learning new skills and making progress – this produces a sense of accomplishment
- competition – many people get a great deal of pleasure and satisfaction out of testing their own capabilities by competing with others
- meeting new people and making friends
- to live longer
- to improve or maintain their image
- as a hobby – something to do
- to please or to copy parents/role models
- as a job or vocation
- to enjoy yourself!

Fig 8.1 Physical activity can help with making friends

 ACTIVITY 1

TASK
List the reasons that you get involved in physical activity or sport. Identify some of the barriers that get in the way of your participation.

CHALLENGE
Choose two barriers for participation and suggest possible strategies that could be used to help lower them and increase participation in a physical activity.

REASONS FOR NON-PARTICIPATION IN PHYSICAL ACTIVITY

In all age groups there are people who do not participate in physical activity or follow an active, healthy lifestyle. More and more people are now obese and there is an increase in diseases linked to poor lifestyle such as diabetes type 2, some cancers and cardiovascular disease.

The main reasons for not participating are:

- health problems
- disability
- injury
- reliance on cars and other technologies
- lack of time and other pressures
- lack of opportunity and access to facilities
- lack of money
- discrimination
- peer pressure
- cultural factors
- lack of confidence and self-esteem
- lack of encouragement and positive role models.

The main providers for physical activities and sports development activities are:

- national organisations – for example: Sport England; SportscoachUK; Youth Sports Trust
- local authorities
- governing bodies – these may be international, national, regional or local
- voluntary organisations
- private sector
- professional providers.

ROLE OF THE LOCAL AUTHORITY

Make sure you can describe the role of the local authority in promoting participation, leading or officiating in physical activities.

Local authorities recognise the benefits of developing physical activity and sport for their community. They follow the national lead in developing physical activities and sport in order to promote healthy living and a better quality of life, and to create a feeling of community. Local authorities analyse participation rates in their area and target their resources and expertise towards rectifying imbalances. This local approach under a national umbrella is intended to ensure inclusion. In other words, to try to include people in physical activities and sport rather than to exclude them from participating.

Sports development

Local authority sports-development policies use a variety of methods to promote and develop sport at all levels. Local authorities will support local schools and colleges with help and advice from sports development officers, who are experts in a particular sporting area. These officers can help schools and colleges increase their participation rates and improve their coaching expertise. Local authorities often run coach education programmes for all levels of prospective coaches. To increase participation and interest in sport they run 'taster sessions', summer school, competitions and tournaments in a wide variety of sports.

Local authorities also provide financial assistance to local organisations for development of sports facilities, as well as advice regarding strategy or matters such as building regulations.

These sports development methods are often targeted at the groups of people we identified earlier, including disaffected youth, to encourage social inclusion.

PRACTICAL APPLICATIONS

BIRMINGHAM CITY COUNCIL SPORTS DEVELOPMENT
Sports Development Officers are personally involved in providing daily and weekly sessions in a wide range of sports, delivering new opportunities and maintaining community sports activities around the City.

The City Council is committed to increasing opportunity for people from under represented groups within the community. Women and girls, people from ethnic minority groups and people with disabilities are a focus at all levels of sports development work.

The City Council set out to increase participation and develop sporting skills and they recognise that this requires committed, well-trained coaches, teachers and instructors. They are involved in the organisation of a wide range of courses and seminars for coaches at all levels. Particular emphasis is placed on vocational qualifications through links with Governing Bodies of sport, colleges and training agencies.

The City Council views sports development as working with others to form partnerships. The council works with voluntary organisations and statutory bodies to develop sport and events of special interest for the people of Birmingham. There is a network of strong partnerships, working together with voluntary sporting organisations. Key partners include: The Sports Council, National Coaching Foundation, The Central Council for Physical Recreation, Governing Bodies of Sport, the Birmingham Sports Advisory Council and several organisations within the business community of Birmingham.

Sports Development
1 Foundation
Work in association with clubs and schools developing sporting skills with primary school-age children. The acquisition of good exercise habits provides a basis for personal development and future participation in sport.
2 Participation
Sports clubs and other voluntary organisations are the essential partners in creating a wide participation level for all ages, if only for reasons of enjoyment, fitness or a simple desire to get involved in sport. The development of school–club links and the process of supporting community-sports clubs with the help of leisure centre managers is an important part of the council's strategy.
3 Performance
Coaching schemes are an essential part of the sports development in Birmingham, providing opportunities for participants to achieve their potential and obtain fulfilment and enjoyment from improving their performance. School holiday courses, weekly sessions and close links with local Governing Bodies of Sport are a strong feature at this level.
4 Excellence
The council run sports development-led programmes and, more particularly, they have created partnerships to provide increased opportunities for participants of national and international calibre to emerge.

Sports development officers

Sports development officers aim to improve access to and develop more interest in sport and physical activity. They organise sporting projects and provide information and training for competitive and leisure participants to increase levels of participation through all areas of society/cultures.

The role involves working in partnership with a wide range of organisations to use local resources efficiently and to develop regional and national initiatives.

Specific functions of sports development officers include:

- promoting sport and health in general
- developing a specific sport (in which case they are known as **sports specific development officers**)
- developing disability awareness within sport (in which case they are known as **disability sports development officers**).

Sports development officers often get involved in a range of activities including:

- identifying sport, recreation and health initiatives
- overseeing strategic planning and implementation
- co-ordinating and delivering relevant activities and events
- employing and training coaches, volunteer staff, etc.
- evaluating and monitoring activities using performance indicators
- maintaining records and producing written reports
- attending local, regional and national meetings, seminars and conferences
- checking venues
- promoting events
- liaising with clubs, schools, professional and sports governing bodies
- developing a range of partnerships to enhance provision and support
- managing resources and a budget
- identifying potential opportunities for external funding
- maintaining links with county, regional and national sporting representatives
- working within organisation guidelines, e.g. equal opportunities, health and safety
- occasionally, offering coaching (where coaching awards are held).

A specialised post, such as that of disability sports development officer, may also involve the following activities:

- training and educating coaches, volunteers and facilities staff in disability issues – experts in disability awareness may well be called on, where appropriate
- using information and publicity to ensure people with disabilities are more aware of the sporting opportunities available to them
- organising sport-specific activities
- maintaining inclusiveness on the agenda.

THE PRIVATE SECTOR

The private sector provides facilities, equipment and instruction for physical activities and sport according to local needs. The profit motive leads the private sector to get as many people as possible involved in sport and fitness: the higher the attendance levels at health and beauty clubs, the more profitable they are. This means that the private sector can contribute significantly to sports and physical-activities development. Private enterprise is behind some significant trends in sport and physical activity, such as the expanding area of personal training.

VOLUNTARY ORGANISATIONS

The voluntary sector is the largest in UK sport and is very influential in promoting physical activities. Voluntary organisations have long been the 'backbone' of physical activities and sport in the UK; the professionalisation of sport is a relatively recent development. Volunteers and voluntary organisations continue to play an important role in the running of physical activities and sport in the UK for an estimated 6 million participants. Voluntary organisations range from hockey clubs to rambling associations. The people who work in them are rarely paid and the organisations are not profit-making; any proceeds from their activities are reinvested in improvement and expansion of what they offer. Voluntary organisations rely on public and private funding.

Voluntary organisations contribute to physical activities and sports development by supporting local needs. They promote specific physical activities and sports, for example the local athletics club, aiming to get as many people involved as possible and to attract people of different ages and from a variety of socio-economic backgrounds. A voluntary club such as a local athletics club would run a team in the local leagues and hold training sessions for its members.

Fig 8.2 Voluntary organisations help to promote physical activities

NATIONAL ORGANISATIONS

Governing bodies

The majority of physical activities and sports that we know today were developed and organised in the late nineteenth century. The participants needed to agree rules and regulations for their sports, so they formed committees called governing bodies, e.g. the Football Association (FA), Lawn Tennis Association (LTA), Amateur Swimming Association (ASA), and Rugby Football Union (RFU), etc. There are over 265 governing bodies in the UK. Teams and clubs pay a subscription to the relevant governing body, which in turn administers the sport nationally, organises competitions and oversees the national team. There are still many amateur positions within each governing body, but increasingly more salaried members of staff are involved.

Fig 8.3 Hockey players adhere to rules administered by the appropriate governing body, for example the Hockey Association (HA)

The national governing bodies are also members of international governing bodies (for example, UEFA and FIFA). These international bodies control and organise international competitions.

Fig 8.4 International competitions in football may be organised through the FIFA governing body for football

PRACTICAL APPLICATIONS

THE BRITISH JUDO ASSOCIATION (BJU) CLUB ACCREDITATION SCHEME/SPORT ENGLAND CLUBMARK

This is an example of partners working together to support judo clubs.

- The British Judo Association club recognition scheme is an initiative to recognise and reward examples of good practice within clubs that are promoting and delivering judo. It will also spread best practice in management and coaching across the country.
- An integral part of the BJA recognition scheme is the Sport England Clubmark – a scheme created in partnership with national governing bodies with the aim of accrediting sports clubs that are committed to providing a safe, effective and child-friendly environment for children and young people.

Although the Sport England Clubmark specifically recognises clubs that work with children and young people, the BJA has developed its recognition scheme as a whole club development programme. This means that it is also relevant to those working with adults and is comprehensive regardless of the size of membership, status of facilities or how often they meet.

The scheme has three levels: bronze, silver and gold. Working through the scheme enables a club to provide the best-quality service to members by creating a specifically trained workforce of coaches, officials and administrators. It also ensures the club is best placed to work in partnership with other local agencies such as local authorities to develop judo opportunities. This is an example of a governing body developing its sport from the foundation level all the way to excellence.

Fig 8.5 The British Judo Association is the governing body for judo

UK Sports Institute

The UK Sports Institute is the name given to a network of centres, along with attendant experts, that supports the UK's top sportsmen and women. It is made up of four home country sports institutes in England, Scotland, Wales and Northern Ireland, along with a central services team, which is part of UK Sport, based in London.

The aim of the UK Sports Institute is to provide elite sportsmen and women with the support services and facilities they need to compete and win at the highest level. The services are provided locally, where athletes live, work and train.

The central services team provides a number of services directly to sports. These include the Athlete Medical Scheme, research and technical development, sports science, sports medicine, performance planning and guidance. There is also IT advice, education and training. In addition, the central services team is responsible for the Athlete Career and Education (ACE UK) and World Class Coaching programmes.

The English Institute of Sport consists of a network of training facilities and services for elite athletes, which is managed by nine Regional Institute Boards.

UK Sport

In 1972 the national sports councils were formed and were deemed to be independent from the government. In 1996 there was a reorganisation of the sports councils and UK Sport (or the UK Sports Council) was formed. The role of UK Sport is as an agency under government direction to provide support for elite sports people who have a high level of performance or the potential to reach the top. The organisation distributes government funds, including National Lottery money, supports world-class performers and promotes ethical standards of behaviour including abstention from the use of performance-enhancing drugs through its anti-doping programme.

UK Sport oversees the work of each home country sports council. These are:

- Sport England
- Sportscotland
- Sports Council for Northern Ireland
- Sports Council for Wales.

www.uksport.gov.uk
Full of information about the work and strategies of UK sport to raise participation levels.

www.sportengland.org
More details related for funding can be found here.

 PRACTICAL APPLICATIONS

Sport England is an organisation created to give opportunities for people to start in sport, stay in sport and succeed in sport. Sport England is responsible for delivering the government's sporting objectives. It works on strategies to make England more active by encouraging people to get involved with sport and physical activity. Sport England distributes funding and invests in a range of sporting projects, including the Active Engand fund.

Youth Sports Trust

The Youth Sports Trust was established in 1994 to build a better future for all young people through PE and school sport. The Youth Sports Trust is a registered charity that initially concentrated on providing equipment and resources to help teachers deliver high-quality PE and sport in primary schools. It then expanded its programmes to create a sporting pathway for all young people aged 18 months to 18 years.

The Youth Sports Trust believes that young people have a right to:

- experience and enjoy PE and sport. Through its work with government, corporate partners and schools, the Youth Sports Trust has developed educational resources, environments and opportunities for young people.
- a quality introduction to PE and sport suited to their own level of development. The Youth Sports Trust's TOP programmes play a major role in ensuring young people are able to access quality PE and sport at every stage of their development, from early years through to secondary school
- experience and benefit from positive competition. The Youth Sports Trust works in partnership with the following bodies to ensure that young people benefit

from competitive activities: national governing bodies of sport (NGBs); national school sport associations; The National Council of School Sport; Sport England

- develop a healthy lifestyle. The Youth Sports Trust tries to increase young people's involvement in PE and school sport and supports and encourages them to become more active. It thus makes an important contribution to the health of the nation
- progress along a structured pathway of sporting opportunities. The Youth Sports Trust works to enhance the provision for young people to experience, and actively engage in, sporting opportunities beyond the school day
- fulfil their sporting potential. In preparation for the 2012 Olympics in London, the Youth Sports Trust is working to enhance opportunities for young people to fulfil their sporting potential as performers and as leaders.

English Federation for Disability Sport (EFDS)

This is a national body that is responsible for developing sport for people with disabilities in England. They work closely with other national disability organisations recognised by Sport England:

- British Amputees and Les Autres Sports Association
- British Blind Sport
- British Deaf Sports Council
- British Wheelchair Sports Foundation
- Cerebral Palsy Sport
- Disability Sport England
- English Sports Association for People with Learning Disabilities.

The EFDS has a four-year national plan, 'Building a Fairer Sporting Society', which outlines the inclusion of disabled people in the identified national priority sports of athletics, boccia, cricket, football, goalball and swimming. Boccia is the disability sport that involves throwing coloured leather balls at a target called a 'jack' — similar in features to the French game of *boulle* and the English game of bowls. They are also involved in the development of coach education and training opportunities that are both are accessible to disabled people and cover the technical issues of coaching disabled people.

www.disabilitysport.org.uk
Gives more details of the range of sports now available for disabled athletes.

www.efds.net
The website of the English Federation of Disability Sport, which gives information on coaching and different sports for disabled athletes.

www.youreable.com
An excellent source of information, including lively discussion boards, for disabled athletes.

Fig 8.6 Most people can benefit from participation in sport, including disabled people

The objectives of the EDFS are:

- the creation of programmes for grassroots participation by disabled people
- the delivery of a rationalised programme of championships and events for disabled people
- the establishment of a talent identification system for disabled players and athletes
- the establishment of regional and national training squads for disabled players and athletes.

OLYMPIC ORGANISATIONS

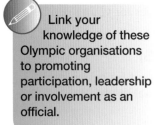

Link your knowledge of these Olympic organisations to promoting participation, leadership or involvement as an official.

PRACTICAL APPLICATIONS

- £265m was spent on Team GB over the last Olympic cycle (from 2004 to 2008) and increased funding has already been agreed in the run-up to London in 2012.

- £600m may be spent over five years in this cycle and may enable us to find an extra Adlington or a new Chris Hoy.

GB team sports made little headway in Beijing, although hockey looks promising. Overall, however, 2008 was a good Olympics for Britain – best of the rest, top EU nation and ahead of Australia. The task now will be to use the values, hard work and enthusiasm of our most successful sports to increase participation for the rest of the population.

The London Olympics is expected to get more people involved in sport – not just as participants but also as volunteers involved in organising and officiating at the Games. There will also be an increased opportunities to take leadership roles, for example, as a coach or in managing sportspeople.

However, official statistics reveal that the number of Londoners taking part in sport has declined since the capital was awarded the 2012 Games. Figures released to Parliament show sports participation in London fell by 3 per cent in 2007, which is the equivalent of 160,000 Londoners dropping out. The decline is in contrast to the target of raising participation by 3 per cent.

 ### ACTIVITY 2

TASK
Identify examples of each of the following roles in the Olympics:
- participant
- leader / coach
- official

CHALLENGE
State why the number of people playing these roles will increase leading up to the Olympics in 2012.

PARTICIPATION LEADING UP TO 2012

A disturbing trend has been revealed in the Taking Part survey conducted by the Department of Culture, Media and Sport, which measures the proportion of people who played sport, including 'low intensity' activity such as billiards and darts, at least once a month. The most recent results show sports participation across the country is increasing, but slowly, with a rise of 1 per cent nationwide overall. The national average participation rate is about 21 per cent.

The government's aim is of getting 2 million more Britons involved in sport by 2012 as a result of staging the Olympics in London. This can be achieved by working with the governing bodies of the major sports. Sport Engand has also been directed to cut by 25 per cent the post-school dropout rate in five unspecified sports.

Government funding has risen by over 800 per cent in the last 10 years to over £400 million a year. Nationally the number of adults doing 3 x 30 mins of sport and physical activity a week is on the rise.

www.olympics.org.uk
Provides details of British activity related to the Olympics.

www.london2012.com
Provides information specific to the forthcoming 2012 Olympics in London.

www.paralympics.org.uk
Provides details of the British Paralympic Association.

British Olympic Association (BOA)

The BOA was formed in 1905. It supplies delegates for the National Olympic Committee (NOC). The BOA is responsible, amongst other things, for the planning and execution of the Great Britain Olympic Team's participation in the Olympic and Winter Olympic Games.

The BOA provides the pivot around which Team GB revolves before and during the Olympic Games. Working with the Olympic Governing Bodies, the BOA selects Team GB from the best sportsmen and women who will go on to compete in the 28 summer and 7 winter Olympic sports. The BOA's role is to lead and prepare the nation's best athletes at the Olympic Games. In addition, the BOA delivers extensive support services to Britain's Olympic athletes and their National Governing Bodies throughout each Olympic cycle to assist them in their preparations for and performances at the Games.

The BOA also has responsibility for developing the Olympic Movement throughout the UK. Great Britain is one of only five countries that have never failed to be represented at the Olympics since 1896.

The BOA is not funded or controlled by government, has no political interests and is completely dependent upon commercial sponsorship and fundraising income.

Olympic organisations such as the BOA help to educate the public about the Olympics and have resources for schools and colleges to use.

International Olympic Committee (IOC)

The IOC was created by the Paris Congress in 1894. It owns all the rights to the Olympic symbol and the Games themselves. This is the world body that administers the Olympic Movement. Its headquarters is in Lausanne, Switzerland. Members are appointed to the IOC and are responsible for selecting the host cities of the Olympic Games, both summer and winter.

Fig 8.7 The Olympic flag

REVIEW QUESTIONS

1 What are the main reasons for participating in an active healthy lifestyle?
2 What are the main reasons for non-participation in an active, healthy lifestyle?
3 What specific social factors affect participation?
4 What cultural factors affect participation?
5 What locational factors affect participation?
6 How can barriers to participation be broken down?
7 What is the role of the local authority in promoting participation in physical activities?
8 What is the role of private enterprise in promoting participation in physical activities?
9 What is the role of voluntary organisations in promoting participation in physical activities?
10 What is the role of national organisations in promoting participation in physical activities?
11 What is the role of Olympic organisations in promoting participation in physical activities?

 EXAM-STYLE QUESTIONS

Multiple choice questions
1 One of the factors that do NOT affect participation in an active, healthy lifestyle is:
  a age
  b gender
  c reaction time
  d smoking.
2 A young person doing his GCSEs in school no longer participates in exercise. Which of the following could be a reason for this non-participation:
  a peer pressure to stop exercising
  b Physical education is not compulsory in Year 11 at school
  c Exercise can stop effective learning
  d None of the above.
3 Participation in physical activities can lead to many health benefits. Which of the following is a direct health benefit:
  a learn new movement skills in sport
  b make friends
  c manage stress more easily
  d raise confidence.
4 Which one of the following is NOT a role of the national governing bodies in sport:
  a agree rules and regulations
  b organise competitions
  c ensure health and safety guidelines are in place
  d make money for shareholders.
5 Which one of the following statements best describes the role of the British Olympic Association?
  a promotes local participation in physical activities
  b represents the government abroad for sport
  c selects the Olympic team members
  d organises the British Olympic team.

Short answer questions

1 What reasons do young people often give for non-participation in physical activities and how would you change their minds?   **(6 marks)**

2 Describe three reasons why it is good to have an active, healthy lifestyle.   **(3 marks)**

3 Describe how local sporting facilities can encourage participation in physical activities.   **(4 marks)**

4 Discuss why there might be an increase in participation in physical activities leading up to the 2012 Olympics.   **(5 marks)**

5 Describe the role of private enterprise in increasing participation in physical activities.   **(3 marks)**

 WHAT YOU NEED TO KNOW

- reasons for participation in physical activity SC
- reasons for non- participation in physical activity SC
- the role of the local authority in promoting physical activities
- the role of private enterprise in promoting physical activities
- the role of voluntary organisations in promoting physical activities
- the role of national organisations in promoting physical activities
- the role of Olympic organisations in promoting physical activities.

CHAPTER 9
SPECIFIC SOCIAL, CULTURAL AND LOCATIONAL FACTORS AFFECTING PARTICIPATION

LEARNING GOALS

By the end of this chapter you should be able to:

* describe specific social, cultural and locational factors affecting participation in physical activities and sport (SC)
* explain the positive and negative effects of factors affecting participation with practical examples (SC)
* describe a range of current government initiatives to promote an active, healthy lifestyle.

> You should be able to demonstrate an understanding of why the following factors affect participation. Apply them via practical examples and remember to make the link. Identify the positive and negative factors for participation or non-participation and then state *why* they affect participation.

BARRIERS TO PARTICIPATION

Specific barriers that are listed in the specification are:

* age – people may think they are too young or too old for an activity, or others have that view
* gender – certain activities are traditionally linked to either males or females and this can lead to discrimination
* education – those attending a well-equipped school may take to physical activity much more readily than those who only have access to a leaky old gymnasium
* family – some families attach less value to sport and physical activity than others, and people from an uninterested background may be less likely to participate than those who have always received encouragement
* disability – if you have a disability you may be discriminated against, access to facilities may be difficult or you may perceive yourself as someone who is unable to participate
* ethnicity – some ethnic groups may disapprove of certain types of physical activity for certain groups, and these attitudes may influence participation
* religion – some people may understand their religion to discourage certain types of activity
* environment – if you live in an area that has poor facilities or inappropriate terrain, e.g. for outdoor activities, then you may be more less likely to get involved
* climate – this often dictates whether a certain type of activity is available. For instance, skiing is harder to arrange in areas where there is little or no snow (although indoor or dry-slope skiing is an alternative possibility).

Fig 9.1 Skiing is more difficult to arrange if you live in an area where it doesn't snow

Cultural barriers

There are barriers to participation for everyone, but for some individuals and groups there are more to be overcome.

Our culture in the UK is diverse and we are proud to call ourselves multi-cultural but in physical activity and sport there are still views and practices that move against a sense of equality. For instance, if a boy who wants to participate in ballet or a girl wants to play rugby, social pressures and stereotypes may obstruct participation.

Here is a sample examination question with some sample examination answers and examiner's commentary.

Q: Analyse why old age might affect participation in physical activity.

Candidate A — sample answer

Getting old means that your mussels and bones are wearing out. You get tired easily and you suffer from illness moor. All these things will stop you playing sport. You also may not have enough money because the old age pension is not very much and heating bills are now ixpensive. The activities on offer at the liesure centre may not be to your liking, such as 5-a-side soccer. There are not many bowls clubs around. You might struggle to get about with your bad hips. You may not live close to anyware that has facilities and there arent many buses. All in all you wont do much at all.

Candidate B — sample answer

Old age may or may not lead to a lack of participation in physical activity. If the elderly person has health problems, then they are unlikely to feel like participating and this may even make their health worse. For example with very high blood pressure it is often unwise to carry out vigorous activity. Old people may not be very mobile and may not have their own transport, making it difficult to get to a facility. They may be lonely and may not know anyone who could help them get to a venue. Many old people do not participate because they don't feel like it. There are few role models to inspire them and they may take it for granted that they are housebound. Many old people also lack the confidence and self-esteem to participate and may feel embarrassed, for example if they were to go swimming they might be embarrassed about the way they look and might feel other younger participants were looking down on them.

Some old people will have the confidence to participate and there are facilities/clubs and appropriate activities that will cater for them. For example there may be an over 60s club that might go swimming or walking. Here they can mix with people their own age and feel comfortable and have a sense of belonging and friendship.

Extension to answer B
Whether the elderly participate depends on facilities, access, encouragement from others around them and their own health and level of motivation. There are many people now over the age of 60 – more than ever before because of improved healthcare – so it is up to local and national government to target these people and up to us as friends and family to encourage the elderly to take up activities and to follow a healthy and happy lifestyle.

Mark scheme	6 marks total. Levels marked question.
Level 1 [1–2 marks]	Candidate makes some points about why old age might affect participation in physical activities but struggles to make any relevant links between the aspects identified and levels of participation. Candidate shows ability to communicate at least one point using some appropriate terminology. Sentences have limited coherence and structure, often being of doubtful relevance to the main focus of the question. Errors of grammar, punctuation and spelling may be noticeable and intrusive.
Level 2 [3–4 marks]	Candidate makes several points about why old age might affect participation in physical activities and demonstrates good knowledge and understanding, making some links between the aspects identified and levels of participation. Candidate shows ability to present relevant material in a planned and logical sequence. Appropriate terminology is used. Sentences, for the most part relevant, are presented in a balanced, logical and coherent manner which addresses the question. There will be occasional errors of grammar, punctuation and spelling.
Level 3 [5–6 marks]	Candidate makes several developed points analysing why old age might affect participation in physical activities and demonstrates excellent knowledge and understanding, explaining the factors that affect increasing involvement in physical activity. Candidate shows ability to present relevant material in a well-planned and logical sequence. Material is clearly structured using appropriate terminology confidently and accurately. Sentences, consistently relevant, are well structured in a way which directly answers the question. There will be few, if any, errors of grammar, punctuation and spelling.
Indicative content	In relation to each of the following factors, candidates must explain why they may lead to non-participation: • health reasons/injury/disability • (perceived) lack of ability/lack of confidence • discrimination by others • low self-esteem • pressures from other interests/hobbies • lack of role models • lack of appropriate facilitates/equipment • inadequate provision in local area • poor transport/access

Commentary
Candidate A

The question contains the command word 'analyse', which calls for an in-depth examination of the topic and an answer with more material than this candidate has offered. Examiners would expect points to be expanded but this candidate lists many of them superficially. Nevertheless, the reasons identified are relevant and include the effects of old age, lack of funds, inappropriate activities and lack of provision/access. In other words, some of the indicative content is mentioned but it is not explored in any detail. The quality of written communication is poor, with poor spelling.

This response is on the borderline between levels 1 and 2 but because of relevant points 3 marks are awarded – just into level 2.

 ACTIVITY 1

TASK

Which level would you place candidate B's answer in, and exactly how many marks would you award?

CHALLENGE

If the final paragraph were included, would the candidate gain or lose credit? Why?

Funding

Economic barriers also exist, with certain sports being out of reach for some people because they cannot afford the equipment, instruction, travel costs or membership fees to participate.

Time

Many people decide not to participate in physical activity because of work, family or other commitments. Sometimes the explanation 'I haven't got the time' obscures the fact that people are choosing to do other things with their free time and not making sport or physical exercise a priority.

Resources

Depending on where you live you may or may not have facilities or sports clubs near to you. This has an obvious effect on whether or not you participate in physical activity. One way of increasing participation for those who do not have facilities nearby would be a transport service to sports or leisure facilities.

Fitness/ability

Some people do not join in with physical activities because they perceive themselves as not good enough or not fit enough. This perception may arise from previous experiences, e.g. coming last in a race or getting resoundingly defeated in a tennis match, or it may be caused by getting out of practice and losing the habit of doing physical exercise. They may decide they were never much good in the first place or are too out of condition to take up any sport or exercise.

However, if someone with this idea of themselves has the courage to try an appropriate physical activity they may be able to overcome this perception and enjoy a more active lifestyle.

Peer pressure

Young people are very aware of their peers' views on life and how to live it. If a young person's social circle doesn't value participation in physical activity it can be very difficult for that young person to be involved. Participation can be sociable but it can also be isolating if the friendship group disapproves.

Fortunately many people young and old do value physical activity and sports participation and encourage members of their peer group to take part.

 PRACTICAL APPLICATIONS

Some activities may have more peer group support than others. For example, a group of boys or men may value traditionally male sports such as rugby and football but may have a lower opinion of gymnastics. A group of girls may support each other's participation in traditionally female activities such as dance but might not be so impressed if one of their number took up wrestling.

Health problems

While there are genuine health reasons for some people not to participate in physical activity, few conditions make it necessary to have a completely inactive lifestyle. Moderate and appropriate exercise under medical advice is more likely to alleviate ongoing health problems than exacerbate them.

Access

The growth of exercise and sports facilities, along with greater availability of low-cost courses, has increased access but some people still face problems relating to provision and opportunity. The following are the main issues associated with access:

- opening times — e.g. may not be convenient for shift workers or school pupils
- age — certain sports are perceived as only being suitable for people below or above a particular age
- race — experiencing or anticipating racial discrimination may put people off joining a particular environment, e.g. the predominantly white environment of a golf club.

Fig 9.2 Racial discrimination may be a barrier for participation

 PRACTICAL APPLICATIONS

For example, in Luton, the participant's ethnic origin seems to have a major influence on the types of sports chosen. Just 2 per cent of Pakistani residents go swimming, compared with 36 per cent of white and Indian people.

- disability – practical obstacles to access for disabled people include poor building design and adaptation, for instance an absence of wheelchair ramps and narrow doorways
- class – certain sports tend to be associated with particular social classes, e.g. polo is perceived as a 'posh person's' sport.

PRACTICAL APPLICATIONS

People on low incomes living in disadvantaged communities in the north of England demonstrate some of the lowest levels of participation in sport ever measured. On average 71% of people from social groups DE take part in at least one sport but in Liverpool the figure is only 51%.

43% of British children play cricket, but in Liverpool it is 3%. In Bradford proportion of children swimming, cycling or walking is less than half the national average.

However, the vast majority of children in these areas have a very positive view about the value of sport.

ACTIVITY 2

TASK

Make a list of *social* barriers to participating in physical activities.

CHALLENGE

By writing a newspaper report as part of a campaign to increase participation and performance in sport, describe the different barriers to participation.

TARGET GROUPS

www.kickitout.org
Details of 'Let's Kick Racism Out of Football' initiative.

www.sportdevelopment.org.uk
A collection of resources for students about sports development in the UK.

If encouraging people to be more active is to be effective and inclusive, ensuring that all sections of society are equally 'developed', target groups need to be identified and strategies put in place. UK sports organisations have identified particular groups of people whose participation rates in sport are lowest.

Physical activity and sport play a major role in promoting the inclusion of all groups in society. Inequalities, however, have always existed, particularly in relation to gender, race and disability. These inequalities are largely a result of historical cultural influences. For example, male-dominated activities and sports (such as rugby, which was first played at public schools or in male-dominated environments), are now played by an increasingly large number of women. There are, however, still very few female coaches at all levels in such sports.

The following groups are generally recognised as being under-represented in physical activities and sport:

- black and ethnic minority communities (BEMs)
- disabled people
- women
- the 50+ age group
- young people.

These are not the only population groups that are under-represented. In physical activity, as in society in general, many individuals and particular groups may feel that they are victims of exclusion or discrimination. Equity concerns fairness and access for all.

PRACTICAL APPLICATIONS

Active Communities is an example of a project that is aimed at increasing sporting opportunities for priority target groups within the population that historically have relatively low levels of participation in sport. Active Communities is a 'framework' comprising services, products and sources of funding provided by Sport England, often in partnership with other organisations and agencies, to assist individuals and organisations to create their own Active Communities. The framework is organised under five core headings, which reflect the most important issues leading to the development of an active community:

- promoting social justice
- increasing participation in sport
- developing community sports leaders
- developing community sports programmes and facilities
- planning for sport and recreation.

Methods of encouraging people into physical activity

Some of the methods for encouraging people to do more physical exercise and sport include:

- ensuring that images and photos used illustrate the range of participants currently involved in the physical activity
- in governing body publications, featuring stories or articles that address the issue of equity within physical activity, from both positive and negative standpoints
- senior figures in the sport and physical activity making public statements about their intention to tackle equity issues
- allocating financial resources for physical activity.

For disability participation, specific strategies include:
- promoting the inclusion of disabled people in the mainstream programmes of national governing bodies, local authorities and other providers
- increase funding
- raising the profile of physical activity and sport for disabled people.

Gender equity

Statistics reveal a number of inequalities between the sexes in sport and physical activity, particularly in the higher levels of coaching and administration. Female athletes made up 40 per cent of the British team at the 1996 Olympic Games yet only 11 per cent of coaches were women.

Strategies for increasing women's involvement and participation include:

- increasing awareness of the issues surrounding women's and girls' involvement in physical activity
- supporting women and girls to become involved in physical activity at all levels and in all capacities
- encouraging organisations to improve access to physical activity opportunities for women and girls
- challenging instances of inequality found in physical activity and sport and seeking to bring about change
- raising the visibility of all British sportswomen.

Additional strategies for gender equity include:

- providing gender awareness training for governing body coaches, leaders and organisers

- establishing a programme of courses that will recruit women into the management of physical activity and sport
- raising the profile of women in officiating.

GOVERNMENT INITIATIVES TO PROMOTE ACTIVE, HEALTHY LIFESTYLES

There are numerous government initiatives to promote healthy, active lifestyles. Some of the more recent initiatives are detailed below.

Healthy living initiative

A published report states that barriers against healthy eating are:

- limited parental awareness of weight status and associated health risks
- parental beliefs that a healthy lifestyle is too challenging
- pressures on parents that undermine healthy food choices.

The Government's Healthy Living programme aims to tackle these barriers through a range of initiatives addressed at families with young children. Young families are aware of the 5 A Day message but are not necessarily eating 5 A Day.

Top Tips for Top Mums

One initiative is Top Tips for Top Mums, an extension of the highly successful 5 A Day campaign, which encourages parents across the country to share tips and ideas on how they get their children to eat more fruit and vegetables.

Top Tips for Top Mums targets young families from low-income backgrounds with children aged between 2 and 11. Recent research by the Food Standards Agency showed that only 46 per cent of people on lower incomes eat 5 A Day compared to 72 per cent of those on higher incomes.

PRACTICAL APPLICATIONS

Eating 5 a day helps maintain a healthier diet and sets children up for a healthy lifestyle. Fruit and veg of different colours provide a wide range of vitamins, minerals, fibre and healthy antioxidants, which can help to protect the body throughout life. Research has shown that people who eat lots of fruit and veg can have a lower risk of heart disease, high blood pressure, strokes and some cancers. To get the best benefit from the nutrients packed into fruit and veg, everyone should aim for a variety of different types and colours every day.

Change4Life

Change4Life is a relatively new movement, supported by the Department of Health, which aims to improve children's diets and levels of activity, thus reducing the threat to their future health and happiness. The goal is to help every family in England eat well, move more and live longer.

A collection of companies including BSkyB, ITV, Tesco, Coca-Cola, Cadbury and AOL have pledged the equivalent of more than £200m in advertising space and services to support the government's Change4Life healthy lifestyles marketing initiative. Major UK food and drink companies including PepsiCo, Britvic, Cadbury, Kellogg, Kraft, Mars and Nestlé have also signed up.

There are also plans for a series of high-profile industry-coordinated public events to be held across the UK in the run-up to the 2012 Olympics.

http://nds.coi.gov.uk/environment/

This will give up-to-date details of government initiatives

www.heartforum.org.uk

The National Heart Forum gives information about initiatives to combat coronary heart disease (CMD)

You will not be asked about specific initiatives because these are continually changing and being developed. You will be asked about the ones you know about – so be able to describe these initiatives and how they promote active, healthy lifestyles.

Five Choices

Five Choices to help you stay healthy:

1 You should not smoke

If you smoke, stopping smoking is often the single most effective thing that you can do to reduce your risk of future illness. The risk to health falls rapidly as soon as you stop smoking (but takes a few years before the increased risk reduces completely).

2 Do some regular physical activity

Anything that gets you mildly out of breath and a little sweaty is fine. For example: jogging, heavy gardening, swimming, cycling, etc. A brisk walk each day is what many people do – and that is fine. However, it is thought that the more vigorous the activity, the better.

3 Eat a healthy diet

Briefly, a healthy diet means:

- at least five portions, and ideally 7–9 portions, of *a variety of* fruit and vegetables per day
- the bulk of most meals should be starch-based foods (such as cereals, wholegrain bread, potatoes, rice, pasta), plus fruit and vegetables
- not much fatty food such as fatty meats, cheeses, full-cream milk, fried food, butter, etc. Use low fat, mono-, or poly-unsaturated spreads
- including 2–3 portions of fish per week. At least one of these should be 'oily' (such as herring, mackerel, sardines, kippers, pilchards, salmon, or *fresh* tuna)
- if you eat meat it is best to eat lean meat, or poultry such as chicken
- if you do fry, choose a vegetable oil such as sunflower, rapeseed or olive oil
- trying not to add salt to food, and limiting foods which are salty.

4 Try to lose weight if you are overweight or obese

You don't need to get to a perfect weight.

If you are overweight you can gain great health benefits by losing 5–10% of your weight. This is often about 5–10 kg. (10 kg is about one and a half stone.)

5 Don't drink too much alcohol

A small amount of alcohol is usually fine, but too much can be harmful.

Men should drink no more than 21 units per week (and no more than 4 units in any one day).

Women should drink no more than 14 units per week (and no more than 3 units in any one day).

One unit is in about half a pint of normal-strength beer, or two thirds of a small glass of wine, or one small pub measure of spirits.

Source: adapted from NHS leaflets 2008

GOVERNMENT GUIDELINES ON ACTIVITY

The aim is to do a mixture of aerobic activities and muscle-strengthening activities.

Aerobic activities

Aerobic activities are those that make the heart and lungs work harder – basically, anything that raises your heart rate and makes you warm, at least mildly out of breath and mildly sweaty. Examples include brisk walking, jogging, swimming, cycling, dancing, badminton, tennis, etc. You can even use normal activities as part of your physical activity routine. For example, fairly heavy housework, DIY, or gardening can make you mildly out of breath and sweaty. Consider a brisk walk to work or to the shops instead of using a car or bus. One report about physical activity stated: 'The bottom line – walking two miles a day can cut the risk of death by half.'

Although aerobic exercise does not have to be intense, some evidence suggests that the more vigorous the physical activity, the better for health – particularly for preventing heart disease.

To gain health benefits you should do at least 30 minutes of moderate aerobic physical activity on most days (at least five days per week). However, you do not have to do this all at once. For example, cycling to work and back 15 minutes each way adds up to 30 minutes. Try to increase the amount to 40–60 minutes per day if you can.

For people who need to manage their weight, exercise should be for 45–60 minutes. For people who are or have been overweight or obese, daily exercise should last 60–90 minutes.

You cannot 'store up' the benefits of physical activity. You need to do it regularly. At least five days a week is recommended.

Muscle-strengthening activities

In addition to the above aerobic activities, adults should aim to do a minimum of two sessions of muscle-strengthening activities per week (not on consecutive days). Muscle-strengthening activities include a progressive weight-training programme, stair climbing and similar resistance exercises that use the major muscle groups. Ideally, the activities and exercises should not only aim to improve or maintain muscle strength, but also to maintain or improve flexibility and balance. A session at a gym is possibly ideal, but activities at home can easily suffice. For example, stair climbing, stretching and resistance exercises can be done at home which do not involve any special clothing or equipment.

A 'session' should be a minimum of 8–10 exercises using the major muscle groups. Ideally, to maximise strength development, use some sort of resistance (such as a weight for arm exercises) and do 8–12 repetitions of each exercise. The level (weight) of each exercise should be so that you can do 8–12 repetitions before the muscle group tires. So, for example, for the upper arm muscles, hold a weight in your hand and flex (bend) the arm up and down 8–12 times – which should make your arm muscles tire.

You can do the exercises one after another to complete a session. Or, you can split a session up over a day of, say, bouts of 10 minutes.

Older people

For older people, the above recommendations still apply, depending on ability. A particular goal for older people should be, where possible, to maintain or increase flexibility and balance. So, the muscle strengthening activities, on two days a week, should perhaps focus on these areas. Maintaining flexibility and balance helps older people remain independent, and reduces the risk of falls and injury from falls.

Children and teenagers

Children and teenagers should get at least one hour a day of moderate physical activity. The hour can be made up from various shorter sessions each day. So, it can be achieved by a mixture of play, PE, games, dance, cycling, a brisk walk to school, sports, various outdoor activities, etc.

REVIEW QUESTIONS

1 What are the positive and negative influences on participation in physical activities?
2 What specific social, cultural and locational factors are there that affect participation?
3 What current government initiatives are there to promote an active, healthy lifestyle?

 EXAM-STYLE QUESTIONS

Multiple choice questions

1 Which of the following may have a positive effect on participation in physical activities?
   a encouragement by friends
   b lower admission prices for spectators
   c more televised sport
   d higher wages for professional sportspeople.
2 Which of the following is a locational reason for non-participation in physical activities?
   a age
   b religion
   c climate
   d disability

Short answer questions

1 Describe three positive effects on participation in physical activities. **(3 marks)**
2 Explain how age can affect participation in physical activities. **(4 marks)**
3 'If there are family members pushing young people into sport then they are more likely to take it up and be successful.' Evaluate whether this is true. **(6 marks)**

 WHAT YOU NEED TO KNOW

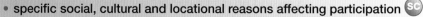

- specific social, cultural and locational reasons affecting participation
- the positive and negative effects of factors affecting participation with practical examples (SC)
- a range of the current government initiatives to promote an active healthy lifestyle.

SCHOOL INFLUENCES ON PARTICIPATION

LEARNING GOALS

By the end of this chapter you should be able to:

- describe the role of the school curriculum in promoting an active, healthy lifestyle SC
- describe the key stage 3 and key stage 4 processes with examples for physical education in schools SC
- describe what schools provide to influence participation
- identify and describe qualifications available in school PE and sport
- describe school extra-curricular provision and links to external clubs
- describe health awareness programmes in schools.

> Use your knowledge of your own experiences in school. You have followed a PE curriculum and have probably also been involved in sport/activities outside the curriculum.

ROLE OF THE PHYSICAL EDUCATION CURRICULUM

The nature of physical activities and sport has developed as a result of what has happened in school physical education. As well as PE lessons, which encourage the development of skills used in many physical activities and sports, a large number of extra-curricular sports activities are organised. Examination courses in PE have raised the awareness of the role of sport in society and there are many links between schools and local sports clubs and other recreation providers.

National Curriculum

The National Curriculum is a government list of courses in Key stages that must be delivered in all state schools from primary schools to the age of 16 in secondary schools. One of the stated aims of the National Curriculum is to get as many children as possible to actively participate in physical activities and sport. Physical education also involves learning information relating to health, fitness and diet.

Key Stage 3

During Key Stage 3 (finishes at the end of Year 9), pupils are encouraged to develop positive attitudes to participation in physical activity and appreciate the importance of exercise in their lives. They are expected to respond to a variety of challenges in a range of physical contexts and environments. They discover their own aptitudes and preferences as well as acquiring and developing skills which enable them to perform competently and confidently across a range of physical activities and contexts. In particular, they learn how to select and apply skills, tactics and compositional ideas to suit activities that need different approaches and ways of thinking. This involves creative development of their ideas. Key Stage 3 pupils also become intelligent performers: they start to understand what makes an effective performance and how to apply these principles to their own and others' work. They gain an understanding of what it takes to persevere and succeed, as well as the importance of acknowledging others' successes. They set targets for themselves and compete against others, individually and as team members. Finally, they begin to take the initiative in a variety of roles, such as leader and official.

The National Curriculum at Key Stage 3 specifies six areas of activity:

- dance
- games
- gymnastics
- swimming and water safety
- athletics
- outdoor and adventurous activities.

Pupils should choose four of these, which should include:

- games
- either dance activities or gymnastic activities (or both)
- two (or one, as appropriate) of the following: swimming and water safety; athletics; outdoor and adventurous activities.

Key processes Key Stage 3

These are the essential skills and processes in PE that pupils need to learn in order to make progress.

Developing skills in physical activity

Pupils should be able to:

- refine and adapt skills into techniques
- develop the range of skills they use
- develop the precision, control and fluency of their skills.

Making and applying decisions

Pupils should be able to:

- select and use tactics, strategies and compositional ideas effectively in different creative, competitive and challenge-type contexts
- refine and adapt ideas and plans in response to changing circumstances
- plan and implement what needs practising to be more effective in performance
- recognise hazards and make decisions about how to control any risks to themselves and others.

Developing physical and mental capacity

Pupils should be able to:

- develop their physical strength, stamina, speed and flexibility to cope with the demands of different activities
- develop their mental determination to succeed.

Evaluating and improving

Pupils should be able to:

- analyse performances, identifying strengths and weaknesses
- make decisions about what to do to improve their performance and the performance of others
- act on these decisions in future performances
- be clear about what they want to achieve in their own work and what they have actually achieved.

Making informed choices about healthy, active lifestyles

Pupils should be able to:

- identify the types of activity they are best suited to
- identify the types of role they would like to take on
- make choices about their involvement in healthy physical activity.

The terminology used in listing the key processes is defined below.

Techniques

These include whole-body skills and fine manipulation skills that need refining and adapting for:

- sport-specific techniques defined by the rules of the sport and its equipment, such as how to strike a ball when using a tennis racket, cricket bat, rounders bat or golf club
- dance-specific techniques as set out in different dance forms
- different purposes, such as running in a sprint race, for a vault or in a dance
- dynamically challenging environments, such as adjusting body position in the air in response to a poor bounce, or adjusting a move at the very last minute to compensate for an error in timing, speed or use of space.

Physical strength, stamina, speed and flexibility

This includes:

- strength to deal with the efforts and loads placed on the body
- stamina to maintain effort (both cardiovascular and muscular)
- speed to contract muscles quickly and slowly
- flexibility to move joints through their full range
- balance to maintain control, shape and alignment
- coordination for balanced and effective interaction of movements
- agility to move quickly and nimbly
- using aerobic and anaerobic body systems
- understanding what bodies can and cannot do as they go through periods of change and development
- understanding the benefits of training and preparing for activity and the types of general and specific training methods.

Mental determination

This includes:

- the confidence to have a go
- the determination to face up to challenges and keep going
- the place of motivation, anxiety, arousal and tension in effective performance
- expressing and dealing with emotions
- the desire to achieve success for oneself and others.

Effectiveness of performances

This means analysing performances, identifying strengths and weaknesses by looking at:

- the range and quality of skills
- the range and effectiveness of tactics, strategies or compositional ideas
- how effectively the body and mind respond to the challenges
- linking these three components and identifying what would bring about improvement and what actions should be prioritised.

Healthy, active lifestyles

This includes regularly getting involved in PE, sport, dance and healthy physical activity. It supports government aspirations for pupils to have at least 2 hours per week of high-quality PE and school sport delivered within the curriculum, and an additional 2 hours beyond the school day delivered by a range of school, community and club providers.

Types of role

These include performer, leader and official. They also include different performance roles within an activity, for example, an attacking rather than a defending role, or supporter rather than supported in a gymnastics or dance.

Key Stage 4

During Key Stage 4 (finishing in Year 11), pupils tackle complex and demanding activities, applying their knowledge of skills, techniques and effective performance. They decide whether to get involved in physical activity that is mainly focused on competing or performing, on promoting health and well-being, or on developing personal fitness. They also decide which roles suit them best, including performer, coach, choreographer, leader and official. The view they have of their skilfulness and physical competence gives them the confidence to get involved in exercise and activity out of school and in later life.

Key processes Key Stage 4

Developing skills in physical activity

Students should be able to:

- improve the range, difficulty and quality of their skills and techniques
- develop the consistency with which they use and perform skills with precision, control and fluency.

Making and applying decisions

Students should be able to:

- select and use tactics, strategies and compositional ideas imaginatively in complex and demanding creative, competitive and challenge-type contexts
- design original and effective plans that improve their own and others' performance
- respond effectively and imaginatively to changing circumstances as they arise during a performance.
- organise and manage the environment they are working in to ensure the health, safety and well-being of themselves and others.

Developing physical and mental capacity

Students should be able to:

- analyse how mental and physical capacity affect performance
- maintain and develop their physical strength, stamina, speed and flexibility to cope with the demands of different activities and active lifestyles
- prepare mentally for successful involvement in physical activity, performance and engagement in healthy, active lifestyles.

Evaluating and improving

Students should be able to:

- critically evaluate, analyse and judge the quality and effectiveness of performances
- make informed decisions about how to improve the quality and effectiveness of their own and others' performances

- develop and implement imaginative action plans to improve the quality and effectiveness of performances
- design original and effective plans that improve the quality of their own and others' involvement in healthy, active lifestyles.

Making informed choices about healthy, active lifestyles

Students should be able to:
- identify the types of physical activity available to them and the roles they would like to take on
- link physical activity with diet, work and rest for personal health and well-being
- make informed decisions about getting involved in a lifetime of healthy physical activities that suit their needs.

 ACTIVITY 1

TASK

Choose one Key process and make a list on the lefthand side of a piece of paper what students should be able to do by the end of Key Stage 4. On the righthand side this gives yourself a mark out of 10 for how well you can do each item on your list. Do the same exercise with two other pupils in your year group who do not take GCSE PE.

CHALLENGE

For each of the following key processes, give a practical example of this taking place in your school:
- developing skills (e.g. teaching hockey skills)
- making and applying decisions (a pupil umpiring a netball match in a PE lesson)
- developing physical and mental capacity (pupil as leader running a year 8 football session)
- evaluating and improving (a fellow pupil assessing your performance in gymnastics)
- making informed decisions about lifestyle (in a GCSE theory session, being taught about healthy eating).

OTHER SCHOOL INFLUENCES ON PARTICIPATION

Examination courses/related qualifications

Many schools run courses at key stages 3, 4 and 5 that result in some sort of qualification (for example, Junior Sports Leader qualification at key stage 3). At key stage 4, GCSE PE or BTEC First in Sport may be followed. In the sixth form it may be possible to study A-level PE or BTEC National in sport.

 PRACTICAL APPLICATIONS

Some examples of courses available in schools and colleges leading to qualifications related to physical activities:
- BTEC First in Sport (level 2)
- BTEC National in Sport (Level 3)
- GCSE Physical Education (level 2)

- Junior Sports Leader Award (level 2)
- Sports Leader Award (level 2)
- AS-level Physical Education (level 3)
- A-level Physical Education (level 3)
- Pre-U Sports Science (level 3)

www.accreditedqualification
s.org.uk/awarding-
body/Sports+Leaders+UK.
seo.aspx
**Gives very useful
information on all
sports-type
qualifications.**

www.sportengland.org/
iyr_london–qualifications
**Here you will find
details of various
awards and
qualifications to help
you further your
career in
sport/physical
activities.**

www.wiredforhealth.
gov.uk/PDF/
GuidanceforHScoordinators.
doc
**For more information
about the NHSP.**

Extra-curricular activities

These are activities run by physical education departments and individual teachers in schools related to physical activities. They are called 'extra-curricular' because they fall outside normal curriculum or school time. They may run at break, lunchtime, after school or at weekends. Many schools run school teams for each age group as well as 'drop in' clubs for pupils to have taster sessions in a variety of activities such as dance, weight training and team sports.

Schools also forge links with local clubs and activity classes. Coaches and instructors are often asked to come into school and run classes. This enables young people to progress into classes and clubs outside school.

Health awareness programmes

Many schools and colleges run health awareness programmes to promote an active, healthy lifestyle to pupils and students. These programmes involve giving vital information about diet, exercise and avoidance of smoking, drug taking and excessive alcohol consumption.

PRACTICAL APPLICATIONS

The National Healthy Schools Programme (NHSP), led by the Department for Education and Skills and the Department of Health, provides resources and support to help schools become healthy schools.
It aims to:
- support children and young people in developing healthy behaviours
- help raise pupil achievement
- help reduce health inequalities
- help promote social inclusion.

The target is for all schools to become healthy schools. In January 2009, more than 97 per cent of schools nationally are involved in the programme and over 70 per cent of schools have achieved National Healthy School Status.

ACTIVITY 2

TASK

Find out the extra-curricular programme in your school or college. Are the classes for boys and girls? Do they involve just sport or physical exercise or do they include other activities?

CHALLENGE

If you feel that there are any gaps in the programme and that some activities or age groups are not represented then write a letter to your headteacher or principal outlining the activities you would like to see run at your school and college and why.

SPORTS COLLEGES

Physical education over the past twenty years has been affected by a huge growth in facilities such as new sports centres and all-weather playing surfaces. In a relatively recent initiative, some schools have become specialist sports colleges.

The sports colleges initiative is part of the specialist schools programme introduced by the government. Other specialist colleges include performing arts, technology and modern foreign languages. The programme is designed to give schools a distinctive identity. Schools must develop partnerships with the other schools, the local community and private-sector sponsors. The government gives additional funding for specialist colleges to develop their specialism.

The objectives of the sports colleges initiative are as follows:

- extend the range of opportunities available to children
- raise the standards of teaching and learning of PE and sport
- develop the school's identity
- benefit other schools in the area, including primary and secondary schools
- strengthen the links between schools and private sponsors
- increase participation in PE and sport for pre- and post-16-year-olds and develop the potential of talented performers.

At the time of writing, sports colleges attract additional funding in the form of a one-off grant of £100,000 and an extra £120 per pupil per year for four years. So not only do schools benefit through the raising of awareness of PE and sport, but they are also financially supported and that is why many schools are seeking to obtain the status of sports college. The Youth Sports Trust (YST) are responsible for the validation of a sports college.

www.youthsporttrust.org
Provides details of sports colleges with case studies.

www.specialistschools.org.uk
Good examples of sports colleges and what they are trying to achieve.

Fig 10.1 Sports colleges must have an extensive extra-curricular programme

REVIEW QUESTIONS

1 How can school promote an active, healthy lifestyle?
2 What are the key stage 3 and key stage 4 processes for the PE National Curriculum?
3 What examples are there for each process?
4 What examination courses are available to school children relating to PE and sport?
5 What do we mean by extra-curricular activities and how can they promote participation?
6 What do we mean by a health awareness programme in schools?

EXAM-STYLE QUESTIONS

Multiple choice questions

1 A secondary school is trying to encourage participation in an active, healthy lifestyle. Which piece of advice would you give the school to help it pursue that aim?
  a Make lunchtime sport compulsory for all.
  b Run teams only for the very best performers.
  c Run sports clubs during weekends only.
  d None of the above.
2 Which of the following is the best way for schools to promote an active, healthy lifestyle:
  a to run a lot of different extra-curricular activities
  b to show more televised sport
  c to give information about the health hazards of smoking
  d to run a drug awareness campaign.

Short answer questions

1 How do schools promote an active, healthy lifestyle?   **(4 marks)**
2 How does the National Curriculum at key stage 4 promote activity?   **(5 marks)**
3 Explain how a good health-awareness programme in schools can promote healthy lifestyles.   **(4 marks)**

WHAT YOU NEED TO KNOW

- the role of the school curriculum in promoting an active, healthy lifestyle
- the key stage 3 and key stage 4 processes for Physical Education in schools
- what schools provide to influence participation
- qualifications available in school PE and sport
- school extra-curricular provision and links to external clubs
- health awareness programmes in schools.

IDENTIFICATION AND DESCRIPTION OF PATHWAYS FOR INVOLVEMENT IN PHYSICAL ACTIVITY

LEARNING GOALS

By the end of this chapter you should be able to:

- identify different pathways for involvement in physical activity (SC)
- describe these pathways (SC)
- be able to give practical examples for these pathways. (SC)

Pathways are routes that can be taken to participate in physical activities and to follow an active, healthy lifestyle.

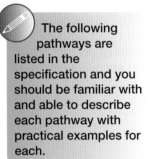
The following pathways are listed in the specification and you should be familiar with and able to describe each pathway with practical examples for each.

Pathway 1 Regular involvement in Physical Education, sport, dance and healthy activity

This involves active participation. It means regular attendance at PE classes with very few instances of not being able to participate. Additionally, you may attend extra-curricular clubs or play for sports teams in your school or college. You may also take part in dance activities and exercise or fitness classes.

Pathway 2 Taking part in school and community sport and dance opportunities

This involves taking up the opportunities that are available either in your school or college or in the local community. Your school may run a number of extra-curricular activities, clubs and classes, and your local community may run classes of various kinds in the evenings or at weekends. There may also be opportunities to be involved with sports such as 5 a side football or netball, or keep-fit classes such as body pump or dance exercise.

ACTIVITY 1

TASK

Find out what physical activity opportunities are available in your local community. Make a list and identify any classes/clubs/sports that are not represented.

CHALLENGE

Write a report on how you would increase the opportunities for young people to be involved in physical activities in your area. Take into account what is already possible and try to give suggestions to plug the gaps.

Pathway 3 Deciding to become a performer, leader or official and working towards qualification

Coaching badges and awards for participation, for example in swimming, are often available as ways in which you can be involved in physical activities. This accreditation (gaining qualifications) can really motivate people to be involved in physical activities.

Pathway 4 Being involved in increasingly complex and challenging tasks and activities

When you are involved in physical activities you may wish to go further as you gain experience. This pathway involves pushing yourself and taking up personal challenges. This can be very motivating and rewarding but you have to be careful that the goals you set yourself are realistic. Over-ambitious goals may lead you to feel discouraged if you don't achieve them, and this carries the risk that you will give up altogether.

Pathway 5 Reaching the highest possible standards of involvement in physical activity

This pathway again is about challenge for you as an individual so that you can reach your potential in physical activity. Whatever role you choose, be it as a participant, a leader or an official, you can strive to be better at what you do and raise your own personal standards. This path will potentially give you a great sense of achievement but, again, you have to be realistic given your own ability, the time you have available and the resources at your disposal.

Pathway 6 Pursuing routes into sport through volunteering

This pathway involves some research into what might be available to you as a volunteer. There are many roles you can play, especially in helping to organise and lead activities. You may wish to volunteer and help within your school – perhaps with lower school activities – or in your local community, perhaps by helping a local care home for the elderly to run activities that encourage more activity for residents. Another possibility is volunteering in national and international competitions.

www.volunteering.org.uk/
Some excellent information about volunteering opportunities in a range of different activities and localities.

www.london2012.com/get-involved/volunteering/
Offers information about volunteering for the 2012 Olympics in London.

PRACTICAL APPLICATIONS

VOLUNTEERING FOR 2012 OLYMPICS

Up to 70,000 volunteers will be needed to help put on the London 2012 Olympic and Paralympic Games. The programme will aim to encourage a wide range of people to join in. Training will be provided to make sure volunteers' skills are of the highest standard.

London 2012 is an opportunity to inspire everyone to develop their interests and volunteer – in sport and also more widely within their community.

Starting in 2010, volunteers will be recruited from across the UK – from a range of communities and backgrounds.

Each successful applicant will have a specific role, allowing them to contribute meaningfully to the Games.

There will be two kinds of Games volunteer – specialist and generalist. Specialist volunteers will have specific existing skills or qualifications required by the role – for example, sport or medical training. Generalist volunteers will not need any special skills or qualifications and will receive full training. They might be given roles in areas such as event services, uniform distribution and Village operations.

ACTIVITY 2

TASK

Research possible volunteer opportunities in sport in your area. Make a poster that will help to inform other people about the opportunities for volunteering in sport.

CHALLENGE

Plan and carry out a volunteer activity. Identify what you should do to volunteer and for what activity. Then plan to carry out a short period of volunteering from either one day up to one week in your holidays.

After your period of volunteering write a short report of your experiences to be published in your school/college magazine/website.

 REVIEW QUESTIONS

1 What different pathways are there for participating in physical activities?
2 What pathways are normally associated with schools?
3 What pathways are often available in the community?
4 What examples are there for a volunteering pathway?

 EXAM-STYLE QUESTIONS

Multiple choice questions

1 Which of the following is a pathway associated with an official?
   a to be the best performer
   b to lead a team effectively
   c to gain a qualification
   d to make as much money as possible

2 Which of the following is an example of a volunteer pathway?
   a playing for the school team
   b being a table official in your school basketball game
   c getting a part-time paid job at the local gym
   d taking a coaching qualification

Short answer questions

1 Describe three different pathways for involvement in physical activity in your school/college. **(6 marks)**
2 Explain how volunteering can be an effective pathway for involvement in physical activity. **(4 marks)**
3 Explain what community involvement in physical activity might involve. **(5 marks)**

 WHAT YOU NEED TO KNOW

- the different pathways for involvement in physical activity
- a description of these pathways
- practical examples for these pathways.

INDEX